MATTHEW, LUKE & MARK

THE GRIESBACH SOLUTION TO THE SYNOPTIC QUESTION

VOLUME ONE

Matthew, Luke & Mark

Bernard Orchard
OSB

KOINONIA PRESS
Manchester

Koinonia Press
19 Langdale Drive, Bury,
Greater Manchester, England

ISBN 0 86088 009 5

© Bernard Orchard OSB, 1976

First Edition: 1976
Second Printing: 1976
Second Edition: 1977

Contents

Preface	vii

PART ONE : THE APPROACH TO THE PROBLEM

1. The Nature of the Problem	3
2. The Historical Evolution of the Synoptic Problem	7
3. The Multi-Document Hypothesis and the Griesbach Hypothesis	11
4. The Correct Methodology	21
5. The Unit Structure of the Synoptic Gospels	28

PART TWO : LUKE AND MATTHEW

6. The Similarities	39
7. The Dissimilarities	47
8. Some Examples of the Luke-Matthew Relationship	54

PART THREE : MARK & LUKE-WITH-MATTHEW

9. How Mark Relates to Luke-with-Matthew: Sequence-agreements and Displacements	72
10. The Imprint of Luke-Matthew on Mark	85
11. Some Examples of the Influence of Luke and Matthew on Mark	91
12. The Markan Omissions	110

CONCLUSION

13. Summary of the Whole Argument   117
14. Matthew, Luke & Mark   120

Footnotes   123
Select Bibliography   142
Index of Authors   147
Charts   148

PREFACE

This book is the fulfilment of a long-standing ambition, viz. to follow up the work begun over forty years ago by Dom John Chapman, and continued by Bishop B. C. Butler and then by Professor William R. Farmer, all of whom I have known and revered, and in whose debt I have been, and still remain, in more ways than one. For them, and for me too, the Two-Document Hypothesis and the Priority of Mark are still only hypotheses, not infallible dogmas; and they have stood secure for so long chiefly because no one has been able to offer any satisfactory alternative.

My aim is to build on the work of these scholars, and many others, in such a way as to create a new, positive and credible theory of the Synoptic Gospel relationships — a theory that takes account not only of the literary data of the Gospels themselves, but also of the biblical, liturgical and historical developments of the past century, bringing them all into a harmonious unity. And though the modern Griesbach Theory reverses the current notions about the Synoptic relationships, it at least agrees in affirming that the Gospel of Mark still remains in one respect the most important of all — in that it harmonises and sits in judgment on Luke's re-presentation of the Gospel of Matthew.

A new theory of Synoptic origins, that contradicts the existing consensus, cannot hope for success unless it is able to synthesise all the existing data into an alternative hypothesis that can be seen to be plausible and possible. In any case the problem is too vast to be dealt with in a single volume. Hence the present work is the first of three volumes.

In Volume I here presented there are three Parts.

Part I seeks to restate briefly the whole problem in the light of first principles, whilst taking careful note of all that has been achieved hitherto.

Part II makes a fresh comparison of Luke with Matthew, and explains the mechanics of Luke's process of first 'unscrambling' Matthew and then putting it together again in a somewhat different pattern.

Part III relates Mark to this newly discovered Nexus between Luke and Matthew.

A final chapter suggests that this Nexus provides the reason why there are just three Synoptic Gospels, and no more.

Volume II and Volume III will follow as soon as possible.

Volume II will consist of a new Greek Synopsis, worked out on the Griesbachian principles established in Volume I, thus illustrating the New Griesbach Hypothesis.

Volume III will set out in some detail the Theory of Synoptic Origins suggested by the new presentation of the literary evidence.

Although this first volume is the result of nearly five years' research, I am fully aware that it is no more than a *documento di base,* and that further research will still be needed in every direction to amplify and to regulate its provisional conclusions.

However the time has arrived when it is necessary to publish at least the preliminary results achieved and to submit them to the good judgment of all those scholars and students interested in the solution of a problem that underlies, indeed is basic to, all the developments of biblical theology over the past fifty years. At the same time I must make it clear that the views here expressed are entirely my own, though I have consulted many in the process of clarifying them.

Nevertheless before concluding this preface I must first express my deepest gratitude to Professor William R. Farmer for repeated reading of my typescript and for all the assistance, knowledge, experience and personal kindness that he has put without stint at my disposal. I also wish to thank my fellow monks at the international Benedictine Abbey of St Anselm on the Aventine and my colleagues at the Beda College in Rome for their interest and tolerance. I also wish to thank Fr Frank McCool and Fr Ignace de la Potterie, both Professors at the Pontifical Biblical Institute, and Fr Conleth Kearns of the Angelicum, for their willingness to listen and for their helpful comments in the course of discussion. Finally, last but not least, I want to thank the Abbot and Community of my Abbey for allowing me time to write this book, which I now offer them as a fraternal tribute of gratitude.

Bernard Orchard, O.S.B.

25 July 1975   *Ealing Abbey, London*

PART ONE

The Approach to the Problem

Part One : THE APPROACH TO THE PROBLEM

Chapter One: The Nature of the Problem   3
1. Introduction
2. Statement of the Problem
3. The Possible Lines of Solution
4. The Origins of the Synoptic Debate

Chapter Two: The Historical Evolution of the Synoptic Problem   7
1. From Griesbach to Holtzmann
2. From Holtzmann to the Oxford Seminar
3. From Streeter to Farmer
4. The Present Situation

Chapter Three: The Multi-Document Hypothesis and the Griesbach Hypothesis   11
1. Summary of the Present Position
2. The Hypothesis of Markan Priority
3. The Hypothesis of J. J. Griesbach
4. Why the Griesbach Hypothesis failed to survive

Chapter Four: The Correct Methodology   21
1. The Difficulty of Taking a New Look
2. The Present Greek Text is Our Sole Basis
3. The Three Categories of Solutions
4. The First Six Possible Solutions
5. The Synoptics and St John's Gospel

Chapter Five: The Unit Structure of the Synoptic Gospels   28
1. Explanation of the Charts
2. The Nature of the Gospel Units
3. The Pericope-Unit Technique

CHAPTER ONE

THE NATURE OF THE PROBLEM

§1 INTRODUCTION

'After two centuries of hard work the critics are still divided between the solutions of Augustine, Griesbach and Holtzmann. This division of opinion is a sign of integrity rather than of incompleteness ... the arguments so far adduced being insufficient to settle the problem.' Such is the dispassionate judgment of a recent surveyor of the problem.[1]

And immediately the question springs to mind: Why has this debate proved so interminable and so inconclusive when so many brilliant minds of diverse nationalities have devoted themselves to it? If a satisfactory answer were forthcoming, the solution of the problem would also be within attainable distance — and there *must* be somewhere a definitive solution, which the Gospels themselves as historical documents could surely give us if only they could speak!

Today the situation is ripe for a 're-think' of the whole problem — despite the fact that probably a majority of New Testament theologians would minimise its importance as a result of their centre of interest having moved on. Nevertheless because the foundations of biblical theology depend in the last resort on the establishment of the right sequence and relationship between the Synoptic Gospels themselves as well as upon their relationships with the witnesses of the Church of the first century after Christ, the question remains of perennial importance. For as Lonergan correctly observes, 'questions of date and authenticity, which might be thought secondary in biblical theology, really have a decisive importance.'[2]

§2 STATEMENT OF THE SYNOPTIC PROBLEM[3]

The Synoptic Problem is the problem of the literary connection between our canonical Matthew, Mark and Luke; what sort of connection is it? Is there a direct literary dependence between these Gospels as we now have them? Does one depend on another, and the third on the other two, or vice versa? In what sequence were they composed, and what were the reasons for the sequence?

There are indeed some very ancient historical traditions in the Church that go some way towards answering these questions, but the evidence is fragmentary, scattered and thought to be unreliable by the majority of modern scholars who have studied it. We shall therefore make no attempt to avail ourselves of it in our main argument, but will confine ourselves entirely to the textual evidence of the synoptic Gospels themselves.

The problem arises from the peculiar similarities and dissimilarities existing between these Gospels both in order and content. Matthew, Mark and Luke have some eighty or so similar units or pericopes in much the same sequence, while Matthew and Luke also agree closely in another forty or so, but in diverse sequence. The likenesses are so striking that all are agreed that there must have been some direct borrowing from one another and/or from some common document or documents anterior to them. The problem is to discover the exact nature of this borrowing.

§3 THE POSSIBLE LINES OF SOLUTION

It is of course only common sense to suppose that before the First Gospel (whichever it was) was written down, there existed in the first primitive Christian Churches or assemblies an Oral Tradition, or Oral Catechesis, about Jesus, firmly retained in the memories of his first Jewish disciples and eye-witnesses; and moreover that some of their memories were soon committed to writing, perhaps in some set form.

At this stage a sharp difference among modern critics comes into view. Some think that the oral period lasted quite a long time (twenty years or so, and perhaps longer) before the Churches began to regulate the materials and write them down. Others think that within much less time small collections of Jesus' sayings and deeds began to be made in various Churches, and that above all a Passion Narrative was formed; and that these collections came before long to be gathered into such documents as the (hypothetical) 'Q', containing chiefly Sayings and Teaching material, and that roughly about the same time — thirty to thirty-five years after the Resurrection — the Gospel of Mark was formed out of the anecdotes about Jesus. Others again think that there were no actual written collections of importance before the formation of one or other of our canonical Gospels. St Augustine of Hippo (d. 430 A.D.) for instance believed that he was summarising the ancient Christian tradition when he declared that the Second Evangelist knew the First and that the Third knew the other two. Our own investigations will later on lead us to conclude that there are some true elements in each of the above opinions, but the question of the sources of the Gospel material itself must always be kept quite distinct from the

the question of the literary inter-relationship between the three existing Synoptic Gospels.

§4 THE ORIGINS OF THE SYNOPTIC DEBATE

The Synoptic Question did not however come to be debated in its modern form until the question of whether there were sources behind our Gospels came to the fore in the eighteenth century. But from the 'Age of Enlightenment' liberal and rationalist inquiries into the historicity of the Gospels led to the growth of the belief that they were not in fact eye-witness accounts, but written up after the Apostolic Age. The line of defence that seemed best to commend itself to Protestant apologists (Catholics were not then willing to take part) was to fall back on the hypothesis that before our Gospels were formed comparatively late (near the end of the first century), there existed not only Oral Traditions in many local Churches, but also some primitive written authentic eye-witness collections of Sayings and Deeds of Jesus, from which our present Gospels were directly composed at the later date.

One group of scholars, following J. J. Griesbach and Friedrich Bleek, while continuing to accept the priority of Matthew, not only advocated strenuously the case for Luke being second to Matthew and Mark third in time, but also thought of these collections as 'the Primitive Gospel' behind all three. But a later group, whose leader was Holtzmann, preferred to think of these collections as the *grundschrift* of our Gospels and that it was composed of two documents, an Ur-Markus, very like our Mark, containing the material roughly common to Matthew, Mark and Luke, and another conjectural source (perhaps corresponding to Papias' *logia* of Matthew), broadly corresponding to the material common to Matthew and Luke alone, that later came to be labelled 'Q'.[4]

The synoptic debate has revolved around these two positions ever since, save that later scholars, culminating in B. H. Streeter, finally substituted Mark for 'Ur-Markus' in the classical Two-Document Theory.

Both schools believed that before the First Gospel appeared, there were clearly defined sources in existence, probably written. These sources have been investigated by the form critics on the basis of the Two-Document Hypothesis, which definitively triumphed half a century ago. It continues however to be asserted by the School of Chapman-Butler-Farmer that the critical evidence offered for the priority of Mark has always been ambiguous and of little value; and this is the reason for the re-opening of the Synoptic Question.

At one moment there were three hypotheses in contention, the Augustinian, (the one officially espoused by the Roman Catholic Church until the other day), the Griesbach (which suffered a decline and a disappearance, which will be discussed further in the next chapter), and the Two-Document Hypothesis, involving the priority of Mark, which in one form or another is the reigning hypothesis today. But while there seem to be none who wish to revive the Augustinian (Mt, Mk, Lk), there is a steadily increasing number who are coming to realise the validity and the potentiality of the Griesbach Hypothesis, namely that, apart from the question of the fragmentary sources written or otherwise, our canonical Matthew was the first written Gospel that has survived, that Luke was the second, and that Mark knew and used both.[5]

CHAPTER TWO

THE HISTORICAL EVOLUTION OF THE SYNOPTIC PROBLEM

§1 FROM GRIESBACH TO HOLTZMANN[6]

The Augustinian Hypothesis was generally accepted by the Protestant Churches as well as the Catholic down to the end of the eighteenth century. But about 1784 J. J. Griesbach, an Evangelical professor at Jena, announced a modification, viz., that the true chronological sequence and the actual order of dependence was Matthew, Luke and Mark. This hypothesis soon became, and long remained, a very popular one in Germany, where it took the place of the Augustinian one.[7]

However, three things happened in the second quarter of the nineteenth century to undermine its popularity: the early date and therefore the eye-witness value of Matthew was seriously impugned[8], the historicity of the Gospels in general was seriously threatened by rationalism, and the Griesbach Hypothesis itself became identified with the 'left-wing' theology of F. C. Baur and the Tübingen School. After 1850 there was a strong reaction by conservative theologians against the extreme views of Baur, and a way was sought to preserve the historicity of the Gospels. A rallying point was found in the work of Heinrich Holtzmann (1863)[9], and from then on the Griesbach Hypothesis gradually lost ground to the Holtzmannian or Two-Document Hypothesis, in proportion as the German 'mediating' school of theology gained the upper hand in the Universities.

§2 FROM HOLTZMANN TO THE OXFORD SEMINAR

For better, for worse, the discomfiture of the Tübingen School led to the rejection of the Griesbach Hypothesis in favour of the priority of Mark. From that time onwards there has never again been a confessional body or a university theological school willing or able to defend the Griesbach Hypothesis, and to provide the backing necessary to sustain it against the massive advance of the theory of Markan Priority, seeing that the latter had the advantage of appearing to support the basic historicity of the Gospel tradition, while at the same time allowing free scope for the development of a liberal theology.

This lack of support for the Griesback Hypothesis in Germany was paralleled in England, and for reasons not too dissimilar. For in England too the support dwindled away for reasons not directly connected with its soundness as an hypothesis. And again its supporters did not have the stimulus of a challenge to develop its full potentialities to meet the threat of its relegation to obscurity. The ideal time for such a thorough testing would have been during those fifty years preceding World War I (1863-1914), when opinion was still fluid and divided; but no reaction then came on its behalf. Moreover precisely during that period the centre of synoptic research seems to some extent to have transferred itself to England where the most powerful biblical figure was the liberal theologian, Professor William Sanday, who had been greatly impressed by Holtzmann's work.

It seems clear that Sanday never made any attempt to evaluate impartially between the Griesbach and the Holtzmannian hypotheses but threw all his great energy, talent and authority into securing the victory of Markan Priority in its Two-Document form in English academic circles, especially by means of his famous Seminar (1894-1910). Its records show that Sanday himself, and the majority of its members, proceeded from the first on the assumption that the priority of Mark was practically assured and that the only real problem was to clear up its residual difficulties (and especially the Minor Agreements of Matthew and Luke against Mark). By the end of World War I there were still a few isolated voices being raised in favour of the priority of Matthew[10], but as the principal university chairs were by then all held by supporters of Markan Priority, the books and arguments of the opposition were politely but firmly rejected, and sometimes entirely ignored.

§3 FROM STREETER TO FARMER

The publication of B. H. Streeter's *The Four Gospels* in 1924 virtually marked the end of the struggle for the time being, at least in the English-speaking world, and for nearly thirty years the Two-Document Hypothesis remained almost unchallenged[11], until in 1951 Abbot (now Bishop) B. C. Butler, who had been one of the most brilliant scholars of his year at Oxford, challenged the consensus with his little book, *The Originality of St Matthew*[12]. However no notable continental Roman Catholics followed him, because their successful adaptation of Form Critical techniques[13] in defence of the historicity of the Gospels had paved the way for their concomitant acceptance of the priority of Mark as soon as the restrictions which had for long been imposed on them by the Biblical Commission were at last relaxed (post 1943). Between 1943 and the present time it seems almost all the Roman Catholic professors in the German and English-speaking worlds (though not in French-speaking circles) have adopted the Markan Priority, together with some form of the Two- or Multi-Document theory of origins[14]. By far the most satisfactory feature of this change of front has been that the division of opinion over the Synoptic Question, which for almost two centuries ran rigidly along confessional lines, has now undergone a complete re-alignment. For the first time the majority of Catholic and Protestant scholars happen to be basically in agreement on the Two- or Multi-Document Hypotheses and on the Priority of Mark. This being so, it seems to most sensible men that the long struggle is over and that there can be no reasonably doubt about the basic correctness of Markan Priority in view of this massive inter-confessional agreement.

The situation today is however not so cosy as it looked ten years ago. For Form Criticism has now replaced the Two-Document Hypothesis as the main pillar of liberal theology in the Reformed Churches; and this makes it possible to discard the Two-Document Hypothesis if necessary, without however giving up the presuppositions intimately connected with it. For some time therefore scholars have been quietly moving away from the classical Streeterian position in search of a more secure basis for the enormous edifice of biblical theology already built upon it.[15] The first impact was made by B. C. Butler's article *St Luke's Debt to St Matthew*, (Harvard Theol. Review, Vol. 32, No. 4, 1939) which he followed up in 1951 with his *Originality of St Matthew*, which exposed the flaws in Streeter's argument and raised once again serious doubts about the priority of Mark and the existence of 'Q'. He has been followed by Vaganay, Pierson Parker, Léon-Dufour, Farmer, Gaboury, Lindsey and Boismard.[16] All reject the classical Two-Document Hypothesis, but all except Butler and Farmer opt for some form of Multi-Document Hypothesis. Nevertheless in most academic circles in Europe and America there is still little disposition to question the priority of Mark.

§4 THE PRESENT SITUATION

Then in 1964 Professor William R. Farmer published his book, *The Synoptic Problem*, which was for the most part ignored by the main organs of biblical opinion at the time of its publication, but which has recently been described by Walter Wink, of Union Theological Seminary, as having historic significance, because it has succeeded in 'demolishing the theoretical basis of the Two-Document Hypothesis as definitively formulated by Streeter . . . Either Farmer is right, or a new basis will have to be laid for the Two-Document Hypothesis . . . able to do justice to all the anomalies previously ignored.'[17]

Farmer's conclusion, after a thorough review of the history of the Synoptic Problem was: 'It is certain that the arguments and evidence adduced in support of the Two-Document Hypothesis are logically inconclusive, and that the priority of the canonical Mark to Matthew and Luke was accepted by Streeter and others not only in the absence of compelling proof but in spite of serious literary difficulties for that view' (*The Synoptic Problem*, pp. 189-90). In the later chapters of this work, Farmer offered a good deal of evidence for Mark's dependence on both Luke and Matthew and for Luke's dependence on Matthew also, but his main purpose was to destroy Markan priority. The present volume aims to build on the work of Farmer, and to re-state the Griesbach Hypothesis in the light of the critical evidence now available.[18]

However, before starting on this exposition, it will be as well to summarise as simply as possible the various arguments used both for and against the theory of Markan priority and the Two-Document Hypothesis and also those both for and against the Griesbach Hypothesis, the two main contending theories.

CHAPTER THREE

THE MULTI-DOCUMENT HYPOTHESES AND THE GRIESBACH HYPOTHESIS

§1 SUMMARY OF THE PRESENT POSITION

In the last decade or so there has been a quiet withdrawal from the Streeterian Two-Document Hypothesis (or Four-Document Hypothesis) position, but there has been no corresponding withdrawal from the most important presuppositions of the form critical method, which originally found their justification in the Two-Document Hypothesis. And as it is impossible to grasp the present situation without a clear understanding of these presuppositions, it is necessary to provide the following summary of the six statements drawn up by Joachim Rohde[19], who explains that almost all modern critical work on the Gospels is based on the following principles:

(1) The Synoptic Gospels are not homogeneous compositions, but collections of small units.

(2) In the pre-literary stage only small units (single stories, short groups of sayings, single *logia*) were handed on in the oral tradition.

(3) When the small units have been detached from the framework of the Synoptic Gospels, definitive characteristic genres can be recognised (short stories, paradigms, legends, etc.). During their pre-literary oral transmissions, the individual genres had a particular *Sitz im Leben* in the Christian community.

(4) The Evangelists collected the small units and strung them together loosely to form their Gospels, the first one being Mark, the creator of the Gospel 'genre'. Matthew and Luke certainly used Mark, but in addition they also drew material from oral tradition (sayings material from the 'Q' source).

(5) The Synoptic Gospels are not biographies in the historical sense, but testimonies to the faith of primitive Christianity.

(6) The Easter faith of the community did not remain without influence on the accounts of Jesus' life. They have been fashioned under the unfluence of the community's theology.

Bultmann and Bertram especially presuppose in addition an unfettered theological productivity on the part of the community.

'It is upon these principles that Redaktion Criticism and modern Biblical Theology have been erected' (Rohde, *op. cit.*, p. 14).

It is also to be noted that while these presuppositions would permit the composition of Mark to be before 70 A.D., they require Matthew and Luke to be some twenty years or more later. The same presuppositions also assume that the various types of stories about Jesus, while being often traceable back to eye-witnesses, were in fact generally shaped by the second generation of Christians, and were freely circulating in a number of Churches outside Palestine as well as within it, during a period of 50 or 60 years after the Resurrection, while our Gospels were being formed.

It is easy to see that the Hypothesis of Multiple Documents has much to commend it not only to those seeking to explain anomalies but also to modern theologians, for:

a) it offers a plausible and imaginative theory of the evolution of the Gospels, from primitive oral tradition via local Church collections of the deeds and words of Jesus down to the finished Gospels,

b) it has encouraged the growth of an extensive and variegated biblical theology, because of the latitude allowed by the theory,

c) it has given almost unlimited scope for theological speculation, because of the gap it preserves between the 'Jesus of Faith' and the 'Jesus of History',

d) it permits any new difficulty encountered to be resolved by the employment of a new editorial process or the creation of a new hypothetical document,

e) because of its fluidity it is a very difficult hypothesis to refute.

§2 THE HYPOTHESIS OF MARKAN PRIORITY

The main arguments for and objections to Markan Priority may be thus summarised:

1) The Order of the Material in Each Gospel

This is universally recognised as having great importance. The classic statement of the Argument from Order is generally regarded as being found in F. H. Woods' essay.[20] The argument is twofold:

i) the order of the whole of Mark is confirmed either by Matthew or by Luke or by both together;

ii) the absence of agreement between Matthew and Luke against Mark with regard to the relative sequence of events.

Kümmel, for example, affirms that 'the comparison of the order of the narratives is decisive (for Markan priority).'[21] The controversy however turns precisely on the point whether these arguments preclude any other reasonable solution. I do not however wish to pursue this point here, beyond agreeing that any and every displacement of sequence, preceded or followed by agreement of sequence, must have rational editorial origin, granted that there is agreement on some form of direct literary dependence.

E. P. Sanders, in an important contribution to the debate, pointed out some special weaknesses in the second argument given above, significantly adding that both arguments were originally developed with the aid of insufficiently sophisticated tools.[22] That is to say, the classical exposition of the Two-Document Hypothesis was worked out with the aid of Tischendorf's Synopsis, which failed to divide the Gospels into sufficiently small units, or with Rushbrooke's Synoptikon, which Farmer has shown to have been framed with the Two-Document Hypothesis in mind.[23] It is certainly true that both synopses make it difficult to see the possibility of any other solution.

Furthermore, the question of what actually constitutes a Gospel Unit was never clearly faced, although much of the argument about sequence depends on where the limits are drawn between one unit and the next. In a later section (Chapter Five, 2) I shall be asserting that any intelligible saying or sentence which is found displaced when two or more Gospels are compared is to be regarded as a separate pericope or 'idea-unit'. Whenever a Gospel editor is found to have displaced one of these, we must assume until the contrary is proved that in this context of literary dependence he did it with a purpose.

Finally, when we come to consider the Griesbach Hypothesis, we shall find that such statements as 'Matthew and Luke never agree against Mark' are quite irrelevant, for it is only relevant to talk about Mark differing from, or agreeing with, Matthew and/or Luke, jointly or singly.

Still, none of this implies that the Argument from Order is invalid in itself; it simply means that it has to be applied in a far more refined manner than the original exponents of the Two-Document Hypothesis realised. Once this fact is recognised, it becomes easy to see that the fuller revelation of the facts makes other solutions relevant and plausible.

2) The Primitive Freshness and Vividness of Mark

This is a phenomenon that nobody would deny, but in itself it offers no proof whatever that Mark was written prior to Matthew or Luke.[24] For if all three Gospels happened to have been written within twenty or thirty years of one another (and, when arguing, this must be assumed to be a valid possibility), then the only thing to be solidly affirmed from the extra freshness of Mark is that the author or editor of Mark had access to a more impressionable contemporary mind, for by hypothesis all three could have had access to whatever contemporary witness (or eye-witness) was available. Admittedly this extra freshness *might* be due to having been written earlier, but is certainly not necessarily so, and this is precisely the question at issue.

3) **The Duplicate Expressions of Mark in Relation to Matthew and Luke**

This phenomenon is easily and naturally explained as the result of Mark conflating both Matthew and Luke (assuming that there existed a good reason for his doing so), though here again it is possible to explain it otherwise fairly satisfactorily, usually with the aid of hypothetical sources or recensions.[25]

4) **The Minor Agreements (and the Minor Omissions) of Matthew and Luke against Mark** [26]

This argument is inserted here principally for the sake of completeness, seeing that it has almost always been considered by the exponents of the Two-Document Hypothesis as the most difficult obstacle. In fact, there is no doubt that these agreements can be easily and satisfactorily understood as showing that canonical Luke knew canonical Matthew, though other more elaborate explanations, usually involving other documents, can theoretically also explain the same facts.[27]

The weakness of all Multi-Document Hypotheses consists not only in the fact that every general argument that can be adduced in their favour can be shown to be double-edged and to be capable of reversal in favour of the Griesbach Hypothesis but also in the hypothetical nature of the extra sources. Hence one is forced to look elsewhere for more sure arguments for the Priority of Mark. Here are three more that have been used:

5) **The Argument from the Hypothetical Source 'Q'**

This states that the material common to Matthew and Luke can be most satisfactorily explained by supposing a collection of teachings and stories, from which each drew separately and without knowledge of each other's work or use (another unproved supposition). Indeed it is true that *if* Mark is chronologically first, *if* Matthew and Luke are independent of one another and *if* they depend on Mark then one is almost forced to conclude the sometime existence of such a document. But if Mark is not the first — and this is what we are trying to find out, and so we cannot presume it at any stage of our argument – 'Q' is certainly not necessary, since other possibilities are available.[28] In addition, if Luke knew Matthew, as many scholars think, 'Q' loses most of its *raison d'être*. 'Q' is in fact as much of a liability as an asset to the Two-Document or Multi-Document Hypotheses, because nobody has ever been able to give a satisfactory reason how such a precious document of the primitive Church – whose exact content is a matter of dispute – supposedly copied by Matthew and Luke independently at different times and places (as far as can be guessed) could come to disappear without leaving the least trace.

6) The Statistical Argument

Various attempts have been made to establish the sequence of the Synoptic Gospels by means of mathematically processing their verbal and literary statistics. The most comprehensive was that of B. de Solages (1959), who believed that he had succeeded in proving the priority of Mark by his method. Farmer however showed that 'his work is in fact a monument to the mesmerising power of the Two-Document consensus' (*The Synoptic Problem*, p. 197). A similar attempt by A. M. Honoré in *Novum Testamentum* (1968) entitled 'A Statistical Study of the Synoptic Problem' has likewise been shown to be unsound by David Wenham in his 1971 Cambridge Tyndale Lecture. Another ambitious attempt has just been made by L. Frey in *Analyse Ordinale* (1973), which will require mathematical ability of a high order to comprehend and evaluate. Statistical analysis is a useful tool, but its value depends on the value of the human judgment that decides exactly what and how much is to be fed into the 'computer'.

7) The Argument from Success

There has also arisen in recent years the argument from the 'success' of the biblical theology based on the priority of Mark, i.e. that it seems to give very satisfactory results in practice. It must be admitted that not a few scholars, though far from all, are quite satisfied with things as they are. J. M. Robinson for instance has written: 'Perhaps the most important new argument for Markan priority . . . is the success of *Redaktionsgeschichte* in clarifying the theologies of Matthew and Luke on the assumption of dependence on Mark.'[29]

In reply it might be said that quite apart from the fact that it is debatable to what extent the success of certain modern treatises is actually dependent on the use of Markan priority, all depends on what is meant by 'success' in this context. If 'success' means bringing the 'Jesus of History' nearer to the 'man in the street', then a great many would be forced to acknowledge that this theology has been far from a success in achieving this end, despite its bulk, its academic distinction and the acclaim that it has received in many quarters.³⁰

The main arguments and counter-arguments for and against the hypothesis of Markan Priority have now been outlined, and we may conclude this section with the mention of two general considerations that do not as a rule receive enough attention. The priority of the Gospel of Mark is very difficult to combine with the known historical developments of the primitive Church, i.e. with the steady expansion from Judaic circles into the Greek and Roman world. This is a much more formidable argument than is generally realised, for the priority of Mark is totally against the historical run of the Church's development. And secondly, the priority of Mark makes it difficult to offer any satisfactory motivation for the production of Matthew and Luke. For it is very hard to find good reasons why any Christian writer should want to re-write *Mark* in the way that Matthew and Luke actually seem to have done. Why did the Church need three such broadly similar Gospels? And why did it cherish these three and these three alone? The Documentary hypotheses have to create very strange pedigrees to find any sort of answer that looks at all plausible.

§3 THE SYNOPTIC HYPOTHESIS OF J. J. GRIESBACH

J. J. Griesbach came to his conclusions about the relationships of the Synoptic Gospels to one another when at the height of his career, and published his findings in a small booklet, which is found as *Opusc. XXII* in the second volume of Philip Gabler's edition of the *Opuscula Academica,* published at Jena in 1825 (the page references given below are to this edition). It was written in the rather stilted Latin affected by scholars of his age and has never, I believe, been translated into a modern language.

Like nearly all eighteenth century scholars Griesbach had been brought up on the Augustinian Hypothesis (Mt, Mk, Lk) and his own theory, first published at Jena in 1789, is really a modified version of the Augustinian view. For he continued to believe that Matthew preceded both Luke and Mark, and its originality consisted in his insight, which he put forward with passionate conviction, that 'Mark when writing his Gospel had in front of his eyes not only Matthew but Luke as well, and that he extracted from them whatever he committed to writing of the deeds, speeches and sayings of the Saviour' (p. 365), subject however to some fifteen qualifications, which he immediately proceeded to outline. The statement of his thesis, with its qualifications, occupies the whole of the first section of his Opusculum. In the second section, he offers three 'observations' in proof of his thesis. His third section is devoted to answering objections raised by contemporary scholars. And in the forth and final section, he sets out various corollaries resulting from his hypothesis.

Griesbach's innovation, or better, his penetrating insight, consisted then in his view that the author/editor of the Gospel of Mark both knew and used — actually had in his hands — our Greek Matthew and Luke when he composed his Gospel, so that Mark depends equally on both.

In this way he established the sequence, first, Matthew and Luke, second, Mark. But he nowhere in this treatise discusses the relationship of Luke to Matthew, though he is aware of the question.[31] We may therefore picture Griesbach's views graphically as follows:

$$1. \begin{matrix} \text{Matthew} \\ \text{Luke} \end{matrix} \longrightarrow 2. \text{ Mark}$$

Griesbach had arrived at this conclusion of Mark's simultaneous indebtedness to Matthew and Luke by means of a meticulous comparison and analysis of the order of units of which the respective Gospels are composed, and he sets out his pattern of how Mark had used the other two in a special table. This table, he claims, shows the following: that Mark

1) generally followed Matthew as his guide, and very closely;
2) at times however he follows Luke instead;
3) sticks closely to Matthew without losing sight of Luke, but couples him together with Matthew, and *vice versa;*
4) sought brevity and therefore omitted much of Matthew and Luke, those parts in fact that did not pertain to the office of teacher that the Lord publicly exercised, e. g. the Nativity narratives;
5) also left out several of the longer discourses of Christ, including Luke's Central Section (nearly one-third of that Gospel);
6) omitted some things in Matthew and Luke that had to do solely with Palestinian Jews and their way of thinking and hence omits many Old Testament quotations;
7) adds a number of items to illuminate the narrative, e.g. Mark 7:3-4;
8) feels free to re-phrase in his own way many of the Matthean and Lukan phrases and formulas;
9) sometimes paraphrases Matthew and Luke, cf. Mk 6:17-29;

10) adds many small circumstantial details;
11) adds one or two short stories 'for reasons that the reader can easily conjecture.'

Now although these qualifications leave much to be desired, his 'Three Observations' call attention to an undoubted phenomenon in Mark, and offer solid evidence to show how Mark must have known Matthew and Luke in order to vary their sequence in the way he has in fact done, whether by consistently deriving almost all his material from Matthew or Luke in a clearly discernable pattern (Observation I), or by leaping accurately backwards and forwards from one to the other (Observation III). He has clearly noted a tangible relationship between Mark and Luke-with-Matthew that can be understood in *his* way at least as easily as it can be understood according to the Multi-Document Hypotheses. The contention of this book is that Griesbach's insight is valid, and exciting, and that it opens up new vistas that have never yet been properly explored. It will be contended in the second place that his theory is incomplete because he failed to develop (because he did not grasp) the true relationship between Luke and Matthew.[32] Furthermore it will contended that despite the fact that his insight fits better than any other theory the requirements of the text and the requirements of the historical situation, yet it failed to meet the many objections that can be brought against it.[33]

These objections can be summarised as follows:

(1) How can the shortest Gospel (also the most primitive in appearance) be the last of the three?

(2) How can one satisfactorily explain why Mark should have left out the Birth narratives, the Sermon on the Mount, the Resurrection narratives, and so on, if he had had them before him when he composed his Gospel?[34]

(3) And why ever should Mark want to make, it seems, a conflation of so many Matthean and Lukan pericopes? And if in fact he did so, why then did he not make any attempt to conflate other material found in either Matthew or Luke separately? How explain such inconsistency?

(4) And what reason can be given for Luke having edited Matthew in the complicated manner that the Griesbach Hypothesis requires?

(5) How can such a carefully wrought theological Gospel as Matthew have evolved soon enough to be the First?[35]

It has to be admitted that hitherto neither Griesbach himself nor any of his followers have ever offered really adequate answers to these questions.³⁶ In other words, there would seem to be as many grave objections to the Griesbach Hypothesis as to the Multi-Document Hypotheses. When such an impasse is reached there is nothing for it but to go back to first principles and to investigate procedures in order to arrive at a sound method of procedure. No real progress can be made until we have found it.

§4 WHY THE GRIESBACH HYPOTHESIS FAILED TO SURVIVE

In 1869-70, nearly a hundred years after Griesbach's Hypothesis was first proclaimed, J. F. Bleek's *Introduction to the New Testament* was translated into English. In this work Bleek had developed and qualified the ideas of Griesbach. Bleek too was convinced that Mark had had both Luke and Greek Matthew before him when he composed his Gospel, because of the comparison of parallel passages and longer paragraphs, because of the contents of the Gospel in general, because of the relation of the discourses given to the facts recorded, and in particular, because of the selection, order and connection of the several sections. Nor in his opinion could the Omissions of Mark be used against the view that he knew both Matthew and Luke, for 'the manner in which Mark is composed, the cycle of events he records, and the order in which he groups them all strikingly imply a knowledge on his part of the other two Synoptics.' (p. 266)

On the other hand Bleek did not think Luke depended directly on Matthew, so that their coincidences 'could only be explained on the supposition that they both had the same Greek document before them when they wrote' (p. 276), i.e. an Ur-Gospel. His arguments for rejecting Luke's direct dependence on Matthew are worth examining, for they help to explain why the hypothesis later fell into disfavour. Bleek writes (pp. 279-80): 'If Luke had used Matthew, then Matthew would certainly bear marks of originality and signs of being the primary document, both in its exposition of details and its arrangements as a whole, and the formation of Luke could be explained by a comparison with it.' Bleek then goes on to assert this is not the case because on the one hand 'now the one and now the other must be regarded as alternately the original and the derived.' For whereas 'Matthew has the more original account of Christ's Baptism, his Temptations, Cure of Jairus' daughter, and so on, and certain more original sayings, e.g. Mt 7:11 (cfr Lk 11:13), Mt 12:42-45 (cfr Lk 11:24-26)', yet on the other hand 'Luke has priority in his narratives, Lk 8:26-39, 18:35-43, and in such details as Luke's one beast, Lk 19:30, etc.' Again Bleek argues that Luke has a more original situation for many sayings of Jesus, which Matthew has collected up on account of certain affinities between them (p. 280).

But Bleek failed to realise that the history of the transmission of the units themselves could be different from the history of the composition of the three Synoptic Gospels. Since his time we have learnt that the units can be isolated from the Gospel context in such a way that it can now be seen that what is certainly a more primitive version of a unit in one Gospel in no way argues for this Gospel itself being composed sooner than a less primitive version in another Gospel. Bleek must surely be pardoned for being misled because only when the era of form criticism arrived (post 1920) was it possible to be sure that an earlier form of a story could easily appear in a later document. Not possessing this advantage Bleek could not but seek to resolve his dilemma by concluding (p. 281) 'that Matthew and Luke were both preceded by an earlier written Gospel narrative, giving the history connectedly and substantially according to the same pattern or type as their Gospels, and that this formed the basis of their respective narratives.' Bleek then attempted to find support for his Ur-Gospel by means of the historical evidence.

Bleek's fundamental error was to assume that 'if Luke had used Matthew, then Matthew would *certainly* bear marks of originality and signs of being the earlier document' (pp. 279-80). But in fact it does not follow that Matthew's units had to have the more original form, and consequently he did not look for the correct signs of Matthew's priority. In other words, Bleek applied criteria of source criticism to material whose explanation lay in the future through form criticism. This failure to clear up the relationship between Luke and Matthew left the way wide open for the 'Q' hypothesis in its various forms that has dogged the Synoptic Question to this day.

CHAPTER FOUR

THE CORRECT METHODOLOGY

§1 THE DIFFICULTY OF TAKING A NEW LOOK

We must first realise that the acceptance of the Priority of Mark has created some basic attitudes and/or pre-judgments of which we must take full account if we wish to come to grips with our problem in a new way. We must realise that from the point of view of a new investigation *ab initio*, these attitudes and judgments, unless great circumspection is observed, are already 'mental hang-ups' or obstacles which must prejudice the evaluation of any new look at the evidence. This has been clearly stated by M. D. Goulder in his chapter on 'The Non-Markan Traditions' in his recent work (*Midrash and Lection in Matthew*, pp. 137ff). Here he has shown that the established conclusions of synoptic research have to a very large extent been built up on flimsy foundations. He makes two points: 1) the nature of the primitive Church has been misunderstood; 2) the assumption that the earliest Christian Churches existed in watertight compartments. To which I add a third point: 3) the lack of recognition of the limitations of literary criticism for determining literary dependence.

As to 1) Goulder points out that form critics blandly affirm, without offering any proof, that the primitive Church was not a simple and highly cohesive society in which one set of traditions would conceivably dominate, but that it must have been a disorganised and scattered body, its mission proceeding by private initiative (p. 138). 'As each man remembered or had been told traditions of Jesus, so they would be passed on and treasured in this community or that. . . . Vagueness is inescapable in our picture of the development of the tradition.' Goulder continues, 'I have called this an *a priori* argument because it is based not on the evidence of the text nor of any tradition about the text, but upon what we should expect, what must have been' (p. 138). On the contrary, says Goulder, the Non-Marcan Traditions of Matthew must have nearly all, if not all, come from Peter, James and John, at least indirectly (p. 144).

Some years ago B. Gerhardsson (*Memory and Manuscript*, p 10) pointed out that Dibelius and Bultmann argue in a circle: 'The form critics built their own house, and consolidated on their own tradition.

It is easy to defend a tradition, if, when discussing the situation of the early Church, one can be allowed to argue from one's own concept of the character of the Gospel material, and to meet theories on the origins of the Gospel material from one's own notion of the situation of the early Church.' On an earlier page (p. 9), Gerhardsson quotes Bultmann as admitting he created 'his own picture — albeit a provisional one — of the early Christian fellowship and its history' (*Geschichte*, 4th ed., p. 55ff). 'For Bultmann the early Church was a sort of "pneumatic democracy" in which spiritual material (*geistliches Gut*) was produced from among an anonymous folk-mass and stabilised in certain sociologically determined styles and forms.' But more recent research is surely right in holding that for all its 'enthusiasm' the primitive Church 'was both ordered and organised, and that it recognised some men — and not others — as doctrinal authorities. It is therefore hardly realistic today to maintain that the Twelve and other leading doctrinal authorities played little or no part in the shaping of the tradition about Christ', nor is it likely that 'the Apostles were ... ignorant, romantic and shadowy figures, lacking any rationally understandable competence' (p.12). And though these views are no longer held today in such an extreme form, the effects of them still sometimes remain in the way in which the Gospel texts are viewed.

As to 2), 'the watertight compartment view of the Christian Churches', to use Goulder's phrase, this is clean contrary to the picture presented in the Letters of Paul where communication between the Churches is both rapid and frequent and in which the views of different teachers are constantly being compared, cf. I Cor 1:12. The corollary is that any apostolic writing would be in immediate demand everywhere, and *a fortiori* any new Gospel. It is up to those who deny this to give their reasons.

There is a third mental 'block' which is best noted at this point, namely, a failure to recognise the limitations of literary criticism for the solution of the synoptic problem.

It is wrong to assume, as so many source critics do, that each evangelist put down in his Gospel everything that he knew about any given anecdote. All one may reasonably assume is that an author or editor will tell us everything that is relative to his particular purpose; and how often in fact does any author tell us *everything* that he knows about his subject? He almost certainly possesses much other information which he withholds (without telling us) because it does not fit in with the over-all purpose of his writing. And so with our evangelists. But *de facto* many critics assume that every minute discrepancy requires a new source, and that if for example Matthew did not put down something that is found in another Gospel, it is necessary to assume that he did not know it. Such an assumption is gratuitous. But of course, on the other hand, it cannot be assumed that he *did* know it, unless his text can be shown to be some sort of precis, which is hard to show. However the essential point is that a theory of sources that assumes the possibility of Matthew, Mark and Luke each knowing much more than he has actually put down cannot be ruled out of court. In fact any and every theory of sources must allow for this possibility as a matter of course. Hence my own theory of synoptic sources, which assumes that Matthew could have known much of what Luke and Mark add to his text, cannot be denied at least as much probability as the opposite school of thought. One example must suffice.

In the story of the Healing of the Paralytic (Mt 9:1-8 = Lk 5:17-26 = Mk 2:1-12), we find that Luke has the men taking the 'tiles' off the roof, and no known Palestinian village house has a tiled roof (so far as we know). Now many source critics would argue that Luke must be amending a non-Matthean source (since Matthew does not even mention a house), and Mark must have another source which is not Luke ('tiles') or Matthew (no 'house'). Thus Matthew draws on Source A, Luke draws on Source B, and Mark draws on Source C. And they would conclude that as Luke has almost all of Mark's story except his amendment about 'tiles', he must have borrowed from Mark and amended him; and that Matthew, who does not even have a 'house', has made a precis of Mark.

But this is far from being the only reasonable way of understanding the phenomena. For:

1) Why should Matthew want to make such a precis, leaving out all the interesting details shared by Mark and Luke?

2) Even when it is granted that Mark has the true details of the story in its *Sitz im Leben*, in a house in a Palestinian village where only mud roofs are known, Luke can still equally well be understood as modifying the story *behind* his own account (and Mark's), and not as modifying Mark himself, that is, when he prefers to describe the roof covering as 'tiles' rather than as 'mud turves'. (Cf. Luke's substitute of 'togas' for 'fringes' in Lk 20:46 = Mk 12:38 = Mt 23:5).

3) Although Matthew omits to mention that the story took place in a house — he merely says it was *eis ten idian polin* — it does not follow that this detail was not in his source, only that it was not essential for him to mention it.

Thus far no solid argument at all has been offered either for Mark being prior to Matthew or for Matthew being prior to Mark, or for Luke being second to either. And as regards Matthew in this example, if as usual he is simply giving us for reference purposes a number of brief case-histories of Jesus' exercise of miraculous power, he would not be interested in the details of the location, and it cannot be argued from his silence that he was unaware that a source existed that said the encounter took place in 'the house', for this was a detail that added nothing directly to the force of the illustration. In other words, most, if not all, of the material in Luke and Mark could perfectly well have been known to Matthew, i.e. it could have been in Matthew's own source, but he did not use it because it did not suit his purpose to do so. Hence one cannot argue that Luke did not know Matthew on the ground that the latter does not mention the house.

Luke on the other hand has considerably expanded the narrative as found in Matthew but in such a way as to fit in perfectly with everything that Matthew has narrated. In other words, Luke, in addition to making further research, could have used the source behind Matthew in the light of Matthew's text in an intelligent way and inserted more detail. It would be the best reason for repeating the story. (And there is no reason why this source should not have been the basic Palestinian tradition deriving ultimately from Peter, James and John.)

Thus we see that the problem of 'house' or 'no house', of 'tiles' or 'turf roof' admits of more than one adequate explanation. Each critic will use these data in a different manner according to his predetermined view of the Gospel sequences. In other words, the problem of the relationships of the Gospels to one another is quite distinct from the problem of the relationships of the respective sources of each story. Literary criticism will argue to different conclusions according to the different presuppositions with which it starts. Without therefore denying the importance and value of literary criticism in general, we assert that it is only a subsidiary tool when it comes to solving the synoptic problem. To obtain any worthwhile result it is essential to look at the problem in a much wider perspective.

§2 THE PRESENT GREEK TEXT IS OUR SOLE BASIS

It is a truism to say that the use of the correct methodology is not only the ideal way but also the only sure way, of reaching a final solution of the Synoptic Problem. The impasse described in the last chapter could only have been reached because somewhere along the line of procedure a wrong turning was made that has led to the stalemate, which in consequence has brought about a general cynicism as to the possibility of ever arriving at a definite solution. At present, despite all that has been written, there exist only hypotheses of greater or lesser probability; in fact the more material that becomes available, the further any certainty recedes. The only possible way out of the maze is to retrace one's path to the entrance and start again.

We begin with a *tabula rasa*, with a 'clean slate', and intend to proceed from the known to the unknown, and never to posit the unknown unless we have to. The canons of literary criticism join with those of common sense to recommend us first to survey the total field of possible solutions, to start with the simplest and most elementary, and to exhaust these before proceeding to the more complicated and the hypothetical.

One misconception that must be removed at once is this: we are not here concerned with the sources of the Gospel material, but simply with the problem of the mutual relationships of the three Synoptic Gospels in the form in which they have come down to us, i.e. whether, and if so how, one Gospel has been the model for the other. That is to say that we are not concerned with the history of the formation of the individual pericopes of these Gospels, nor with an Ur-Matthew or an Ur-Mark or an Ur-Luke, i.e. a supposed intermediate stage in the formation of the Gospel tradition. Undoubtedly, we may later be led to consider such possibilities, but until we have good reason to suspect the contrary we shall assume that such documents — if they ever existed — played an insignificant part in the formation of the Gospel tradition. In other words, we are concerned only with the shape of the Gospels we have. This is most certainly the right and proper way to begin our study; let us see where it leads us.[37]

§3 THE THREE CATEGORIES OF SOLUTIONS

Putting on one side for the time being then all such speculations, and with nothing but the Greek text of our three Gospels in our hands (but of course remaining conscious of the long history and ramifications of the Problem), our first question is: are the likenesses between the three Synoptic Gospels to be explained by some form of direct and/or indirect literary dependence? The universally agreed answer today is that some measure of direct and/or indirect literary dependence is required to explain their likenesses. This dependence must fall into one of the three following categories: *either:*

1) No intermediate document is necessary to explain their likenesses; and hence the first was used by the second, and the third used both, each Gospel of course having its own special sources and also using oral (and possibly even written) traditions already in existence;[38] *or*

2) All three Gospels independently utilised in different degrees the same earlier common written primitive source or sources (*grundschrift*); *or*
3) A mixed dependence, in which one or more Gospels have been used by the third as well as one or more intermediate documents.

§4. THE FIRST SIX POSSIBLE SOLUTIONS

According to the correct methodological principle that *entia non sunt multiplicanda*, the first category must first be worked over and its possibilities exhausted before we pass to the second and third categories, which offer solutions based on the use of either Ur-Gospels or of collections such as 'Q' by the final editors of our Gospels. Now Farmer has shown that there are only eighteen possible solutions in the first category, and that these can in fact be further reduced to just six, (cf. *The Synoptic Problem*, p. 208). These six may be set out diagramatically as in Diagram I.

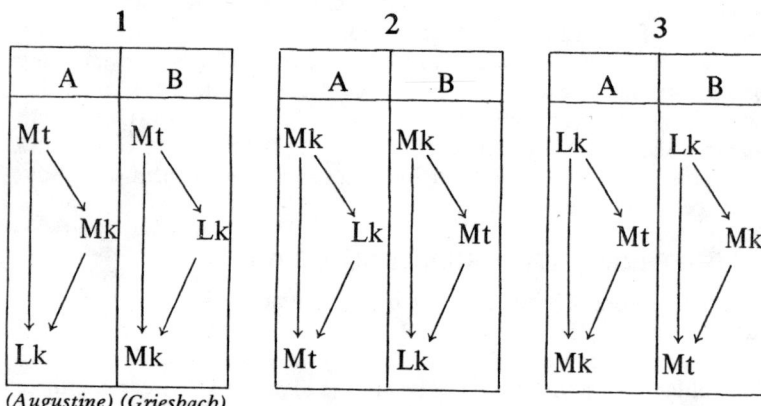

DIAGRAM I

Provisionally, we leave on one side the two showing the priority of Luke, which need be reconsidered only if our research into the others fails to be fruitful.

Similarly we may pass the two showing the Priority of Mark, because these are usually advocated only when there is along with Mark some other document postulated that explains the features in Matthew and Luke that cannot be derived from Mark. (But see §3, 1) above.)

We are thus left with the two possible solutions that put Matthew first, as methodologically the first to be examined.

1 (A) is of course the Augustinian Hypothesis, that has been once more seriously propounded by Chapman and Butler, but which Farmer has shown to be inadequate. We therefore pass to

1 (B) which is the Griesbach Hypothesis, the only solution in this category that has not been subjected to examination during the past century.

In examining the Griesbach Hypothesis, there are two distinct questions to be borne in mind:

1) what Griesbach himself actually proposed in 1789, with its strong and weak points,
2) the question of presenting the main insights of Griesbach in the light of the progress that has been made since his day both in Gospel studies and in the new tools and techniques available.

The aim of the present volume is to utilise and update the Griesbach insight. It is all the more vital to do it, because correct methodological procedure points to the study of the Griesbach Hypothesis as the only remaining one that seeks a solution without postulating an intermediate document.

§5 THE SYNOPTICS AND ST JOHN'S GOSPEL

There is one other position that remains to be clarified before we begin our study of the Synoptic Gospels, and that is the question of their relationship with the Gospel of St John. The position adopted here is the traditional one, namely, that St John is subsequent to the last of the Synoptic Gospels, which in consequence have not been affected by it. On this point we have the support of the recent commentaries of R. Brown and R. Schnackenburg (see their respective introductions). On the other hand, the extent of the influence, if any, of one or more of the Synoptic Gospels on the Gospel of St John is one that cannot be entered upon here, though it is conceiveable that they had some influence on its composition.

CHAPTER FIVE

THE UNIT STRUCTURE OF THE SYNOPTIC GOSPELS

Before we begin to work out the actual relationships existing between the Synoptic Gospels, we must first examine their structure and also acquire some idea of the nature of the units of which they are composed. The best way to do this is to make a comparative structural analysis of them, see Volume II. Such an analysis is of vital importance because, as we have seen above (Chapter Three, §2), our understanding will be largely conditioned by it. For it is not easy fully to perceive the feasibility of the modern Griesbach Hypothesis until it has been set out in the form of a synopsis adapted to its requirements.[39] However the creation of such a synopsis is not meant to prejudice the issues involved, but simply to enable the student to perceive visually the full implications of the new theory. Chart I, to which we now turn, represents in a graphical mode the parallelism of the Gospel Units in accordance with the assumptions of the new hypothesis.

§1 EXPLANATION OF THE CHARTS

Every attempt to construct a Gospel synopsis brings one up immediately against the problem of their 'unit structure', and a practical judgment has first to be made with regard to the criteria governing the size and character of each unit. There is as yet no entire agreement among the composers of the current synopses about the amount of subdivision, and it is certain that in some cases the actual demarcation will depend on the synoptic hypothesis they happen to favour.[40] All the same the main unit structure has been identified as the result of the work of many scholars over many years, though some important points still remain in dispute. The fruit of their study is to be seen in any synopsis of the Greek text, for example, in K. Aland's *Synopsis Quattuor Evangeliorum*, whose unit divisions have been followed fairly closely. Only the primary parallels have been utilised because these can be taken as a general rule to presuppose some literary connection. Aland does not explain the criteria he has used to distinguish them, but in his Introduction (p. X) he mentions that the format is 'suitable for use in academic instruction and scientific research': and we shall be using it for this latter purpose. Presumably in making his unit divisions he had at least the following considerations in mind:

1) the consensus of scholars;
2) that in each Gospel the parallel units as a rule, either
   (a) have a considerable number of words in common; or
   (b) have some common syntax; or
   (c) have not only the same topic, but in most cases a similar treatment of it also; or
   (d) appear as a general rule (though by no means invariably) in the same over-all sequence or context; or
   (e) form an 'idea unit'; or
   (f) possess a combination of these factors.

There are also a few units, e.g. the Genealogies, the Nativity narratives, etc., where the topic is the same, but the treatment quite different. In any case of course the juxtaposition means no more than that there is at least some recognised *prima facie* likeness.

But each unit is seen to be an intelligible whole, an identifiable 'idea-unit' that can be detached from its context and handled separately, and which can, if desired, be juxtaposed or combined with another unit from elsewhere, according to the editor's policy. Quite often units are found together in small clusters which are transposed as a group; while groups of these clusters make up such large units as the Great Sermon. Chart I is based on the assumption that Luke has quarried in Matthew, so that every 'idea-unit' which Luke transfers in fact qualifies as a separate unit or pericope.

Chart I (and Chart IIA) are symbolic representations of the synoptic unit-structure. Owing to limitations of space, the relationships between Matthew and Luke and between Luke-with-Matthew and Mark are perforce represented on the one Chart instead of separately. The Luke-Matthew relationships are indicated by four different sorts of line; the Markan by a continuous hatched line.

The Charts illustrate the direct literary relationship presumed to exist between the main units only. They do not for example indicate transfers of material from within one parallel unit to another, e.g. Mt 8:11-12 to Lk 13:28-29, or Mt 10:17-22 to Lk 21:12ff (these are in fact recorded either in Chart IIB, if they are in Lk's Central Section, or else in Volume II, *The Fourfold Gospel Synopsis*). Nor do they indicate, for example, the Matthean and Lukan parallels to Mk 9:49-50, which will be dealt with in a special note (p. 79).

The Charts indicate the actual transpositions on the basis of the presumed literary connections between the respective parallel units. They are invaluable aids in handling the complex data, and no more. They do not and cannot indicate the direction in which the lines of dependence run, whether from left to right, or from right to left; this has yet to be worked out. Their great advantage is to give a remarkably simple yet basically correct picture of the main lines of literary similarity, and so greatly to facilitate the reader's task in following the complex argument. They avoid cluttering it up with too much detail and confusing the general outline with too many intersecting lines. This is particularly important and necessary with the Matthean material found in Luke's Central Section. Finally to make the Charts easier to read and interpret, the relationships of the units in the respective Great Sermons are shown on a separate Chart IIA.

The following is the explanation of the signs used in the Charts:

1) The initials BO refer to the present writer's *The Fourfold Gospel Synopsis*, Volume II in this series.
2) The line joining any two units means no more and no less than what the juxtaposition of two major parallels means in any synopsis.
3) Since by definition every line is a representation of some link between two similar units, therefore
   (a) where the lines are horizontally parallel it means that no transpositions of sequence have taken place in so far as these parallel units themseves are concerned, i.e. that the units involved have the same absolute and relative sequence in the framework of their respective Gospels;
   (b) where the lines are diagonal and parallel (without crossing one another) it indicates that the *relative* sequence of these units has been preserved during transference to another part of the other Gospel;
   (c) where the lines either cross or diverge from their starting-point, it means that in the transference the *relative* sequence too has been changed by one or other of the evangelists.
4) Four different types of line linking the related units indicate four different aspects of the Luke/Matthew relationship; and a fifth type indicates the relationship of Mark to Luke and/or Matthew:
   (a) horizontal unbroken lines indicate units absolutely and relatively in the same sequence with respect to one another;

(b) diagonal unbroken lines indicate that the same material is found in one Gospel in a different sequence from the other;
(c) broken lines indicate Matthean material found the Central Section of Luke;
(d) broken dot-dash lines indicate transfers where the parallelism is qualified in some special way;
(e) in respect of Mark, the hatched lines indicate Markan parallels with Matthew and/or Luke.

5) Where a plain horizontal line from Matthew to Luke is linked by the Lukan unit-title with the Markan hatched horizontal line, a 'Triple Tradition' unit is indicated.

6) The titles given to the units are arbitrary and are offered as mnemonic aids.

§2 THE NATURE OF THE GOSPEL UNITS

The ease with which the Gospels of Matthew, Luke and Mark divide into literary units of various kinds at once suggests that we are face to face with the employment of certain ancient literary forms which the Evangelists have utilised. Clearly then our next task is to find out, if this be so, what they were, and how they were employed in the first century of the Christian era. Now it happens that in the past thirty years two important works have been published that deal with these matters precisely from the angle in which we are interested.[41] The better know is Birger Gerhardsson's *Memory and Manuscript,* which is the fundamental monograph on the influence of rabbinic techniques in relation to the Epistles of Paul. But Gerhardsson seems to have been unaware (for he does not mention it in his bibliography) of the earlier work of R.O.P. Taylor, *The Groundwork of the Gospels,* which not only anticipates some of Gerhardsson's conclusions, but also explains the influence of Greek educational methods on the Gospels. Gerhardsson has explained how the Rabbis handed down their Tradition by means of Mishnah, i.e. repetition, and how deeply the first Christian teachers were influenced by their methods; for he shows how 'the oral *Torah* of the Jews is called in the Gospels the *paradosis presbyteron* (Mt 15:2, 3, 6 = Mk 7:9, 13)' (p. 288). Gerhardsson aimed to show and (in the opinion of many scholars) succeeded in showing that the first Christians transmitted their own version of the *paradosis*, as received from Jesus, by using the identical methods (cf. *op. cit.*, p. 290ff).

Gerhardsson's thesis in short is that the earliest Christian tradition was linked with authoritative spokesmen, and that the tradition was learnt by heart (*op. cit.* pp. 205-6).

Taylor is in perfect accord: 'We must remember', he writes, 'that for the Jew of that time the only legitimate way of conveying the facts was the imparting of the exact words of the record. Nothing less was required of him, and nothing less was expected by the pupils' (*op. cit.*, p. 25). And again (pp. 47-48), 'The Rabbis taught according to fixed formulae which they had inherited and which they passed on in identical form; they also gave judgments on questions of importance according to the standards imposed by these formulae.' But Taylor's special contribution is to have pointed out that the same method of passing on information by learning by heart was practised by the Greek Rhetors. Thus both in the Jewish and in the Greco-Roman world very similar methods were used for passing on reliable and accurate records of the words and deeds of great men. He goes even further when he writes, 'To the men of Jesus' day oral transmission was natural and normal . . .; whereas we regard any system of oral transmission as a mere makeshift for the written word, they had an actual and decided preference for records inscribed in men's brains' (*op. cit.*, p. 61).

Now the principal literary forms used by the Greek Rhetors as the means of communicating the Greek tradition were five in number: the *gnome* (the maxim or pregnant saying), the *parabole* ('an effort to put an idea before the mind's eye'), the *diegesis* (or narrative), the *apomnemoneuma* (or recollection, the natural artless form in which an incident would be remembered), and the *chreia* (or pithy anecdote). Taylor continues: 'The study of the Rhetors shows that all the constituents of the Gospels fall into the categories of that Hellenic thought, which was the thought of all the Mediterranean civilisation. It is perfectly easy to classify the Gospels by these very terms: *chreia, apomnemoneuma, diegesis, parabole*, in precisely their Hellenic senses' (p. 81). To which we should add, for the sake of completeness, the term *gnome*. These are the real literary units of the Synoptic Gospels, and the other categories normally used by modern scholars and critics, e.g. 'the miracle-story', etc., are not based on these classical divisions, but on theologically motivated considerations.

In classical times the commonest form was the *chreia*, which was intended to be known by heart, and which was thus defined by the famous rhetor Theon, 'A *chreia* is a concise and pointed account of something said or done, attributed to a particular person' (Taylor, p 76). Taylor then adds, 'The *chreia* was a fundamental form (to the Hellenic mind) — not only a literary form, but an historical statement.'

Now while the Gospels contain a certain number of *chreiai* (e.g. Lk 21:1-4 = Mk 12:41-44; Mt 18:21-22), the majority of the Gospel stories are *apomnemoneumata,* or *Extended Chreiai,* as M. Speaker calls them in her monograph (see Bibliography). But the difference between them is simply that the *chreia* was shorter and very concise, while the *apomnemoneuma* was more circumstantial, more diffuse, and therefore longer.[42] Since these two forms, together with the *parabole*, were the principal means by which entirely reliable and accurate information was handed on from one generation to the next in the secular world of the first century A. D., it is easy to see why these same literary forms were used by the first Christians to pass on the teachings of Jesus both reliably and faithfully to succeeding generations, and why they came in due course to be incorporated in our Gospels. In order to convince hearers (and later readers also) of the truth of the deeds and words of Jesus, it was therefore necessary for the first Christian witnesses to put them into the universally recognised forms for transmitting them to posterity.

It is a fallacy to think that the Greek world was gullible and uncritical. 'The society in and for which Mark's Gospel was produced was one which laid great stress on the necessity for firsthand evidence. This is shown by the insistence on the importance of witnesses' (Taylor, p. 11). Luke for instance stresses his own consultation of eye-witnesses, and Acts 1 shows that Peter was regarded as the chief eye-witness of all that Jesus said and did. 'The Gospels are the product not of the collectors of folklore but of a responsible organisation carefully controlling those whom it sent out to publish its news' (Taylor, p. 66). 'Responsible' is the operative word — responsible to see that only the truth was published. Yet the common modern belief 'that for at least thirty years the story of Jesus was a matter of "tradition", has opened the door to the assumption that for that period there was nothing but popular rumour, at the mercy of the dreams and hopes of Galilean peasants.' But this belief is due to a misunderstanding of what oral transmission really meant in those days. For as Taylor says (*op. cit.,* p. 66), 'Tradition, in the first century at least, stood for a system of ensuring the retention of information . . .; though it also meant a written record, it was still more a fixing in men's memories.' Hence the 'traditions dealt with by Papias were not mere rumours or untended memories, but definite statements carefully retained and deliberately issued by responsible persons' (Taylor, p. 71). Hence the Gospel of Mark (which Taylor incidentally believed to be the earliest) stands as a monument to the fact that the 'extended *chreia*' was the principal form by which the Gospel tradition was handed on intact and unadulterated. The *chreia* was 'the recognised means also of persuasion, and the Christian proselyte needed to be thoroughly persuaded' (Taylor, p 76). These literary forms were the first necessity for thorough persuasion; and such oral records once made could then be easily and scrupulously safeguarded in unspoilt memories before being written down.

These then are some of the reasons for thinking that the unit divisions that we shall shortly be working with are not arbitrary, but do in fact correspond to the five types of literary form used by Greek rhetors and teachers of the first century A. D. as the accepted vehicles for the transmission of thoroughly reliable and accurate historical information from one generation to the next. We may also safely presume that Luke himself, with his cultivated literary background, was fully competent to recognise and handle these forms whenever he came across them. The question of how these forms came to be used in Christian circles is however a fascinating one, but outside the scope of our present investigation.

§3 THE PERICOPE-UNIT TECHNIQUE[43]

The assumption behind the investigation we are about to make is that Luke is dependent on Matthew. Whether or not this is so can only be discovered by first comparing the two Gospels, and there are two complementary methods of making this comparison. One way is to compare the two Gospels as literary wholes by examining the literary framework of each and comparing the respective arrangements of the units that compose them. The other is to see the amount of common vocabulary, phrases, syntax and ideas in each individual unit. The two methods are complementary and the one will provide a check on the results attained through the other; but the correct methodology is to begin with the comparison of the over-all plan and then to check with the individual units.[44] The reason of course is that the ultimate and governing aim of the whole work is best discerned by looking first at the whole before descending to the parts, though of course the parts offer clues to the meaning of the whole.

Now the Griesbach assumption is that Matthew and Luke preceded Mark. And since Luke is so like Matthew in some respects and so unlike him in others, it may prove that Luke had a twofold task to achieve in writing, namely to use as much as he could of Matthew, and also to find as much room as possible for the great amount of new material that he had gathered. If so, Luke must have made an over-all plan to embrace the inclusion of both sorts of material. In other words, he will have had to decide in advance exactly how much of Matthew he intended to retain and how much he intended to leave out. This selection will undoubtedly have been done in accordance with the over-all purpose he had in undertaking to write. If in fact he decided to utilise Matthew, it must have been because in his opinion it was already a recognised and accepted work in the same field. We shall have to keep a sharp lookout for all these points and many others when making our comparison.

But it is also to be stressed that our evangelists behaved like other authors. Thus the author or editor (whoever he may be) first gathers all his material together, sorts it into groups, and then decides on the sequence of the chapters or sections of his book. This sequence will depend on a number of factors, his over-all purpose in writing, the literary customs of the era in which he lives, the nature of the audience for whom he is writing, the tractability of his materials, and finally the nature of previous works that have appeared in that field. If there happens to be in existence another recognised and acceptable work in the same field and on the same topic, the responsible author or editor will normally first study the earlier work before finally deciding on his own sequence and method of presentation, cf. Lk 1:1-4. Nor can we exclude the possibility that the author or editor may have been influenced by more than one preceding work and that he will select and combine those features from the others that suit his purpose; he may even seek to conflate common units or to resolve problems posed by the different approaches of the earlier authors. Again, an author or editor may follow the general sequence of the other and yet make little or no direct use of the materials contained in the other. For he may be getting his own material from quite a different tradition and in sufficient amplitude not to have to rely on the other; in any case he may have very different ideas, yet still be anxious to present them in a similar over-all fashion.[45] We cannot know in advance, but we must be prepared to go wherever the evidence of dependence may lead us.

This concludes Part One, our Approach to the Synoptic Problem. The procedure we must now follow is clear. Firstly, we must compare the over-all plan of the units of Luke and Matthew together (see Charts I [less Markan parallels], IIA, IIB). This comparison will reveal their basic similarity of shape, despite many superficial differences. And precisely because the greater number of the main units of Luke are absolutely parallel to their Matthean counterparts, there will be a correspondingly important significance in the actual displacements, both small (individual sayings or sentences) and large (recognised pericope units, whether *chreiai* or *apomnemoneumata*). The discussion of them will occupy Chapters Six and Seven. And then in Chapter Eight we shall see the same editorial process at work within the Centurion's

Servant Unit and in the groups of units associated with the Central Section and the Great Sermon. This will prepare the way for the examination of Griesbach's main insight in Part Three.

PART TWO

Luke and Matthew

Part Two : LUKE AND MATTHEW

Chapter Six: The Similarities   39
1. The Unit Sequence
2. The Unit-Sequence Agreement of Luke with Matthew
3. The Sequence of Gospel Topics, Table I
4. The Explanation of Table I
5. A Review of Table I

Chapter Seven: The Dissimilarities   47
1. Summary of the Dissimilarities as regards Unit-Sequence
2. The 'Switch' of the Parables' Discourse
3. The Transfer of Units found in Luke 4-8:
   1) Units having the same topic but different content
   2) Units out of sequence but parallel and similar in content
   3) Units in relative sequence
   4) Remaining displacements in Luke 4-8
4. The Transfer of Units to the Central Section (Luke 9:52-18:14)
   1) Transfers from the six discourses
   2) Transfers from the intervening chapters
5. Lukan Additions to Matthew
6. Lukan Omissions of Matthean Units

Chapter Eight: Some Examples of the Luke-Matthew Relationship   54
1. The Unit of the Centurion's Slave
2. The First Preaching Tour, Luke 4:44-6:19
3. Excursus on the Central Section
4. Excursus on Luke's Adaptation of the Great Sermon
5. Provisional Conclusion

CHAPTER SIX

THE SIMILARITIES BETWEEN LUKE AND MATTHEW

§1 THE UNIT SEQUENCE

The purpose of this chapter is to pursue as closely as possible the precise relationship existing between Luke and Matthew by studying the sequence of the units of which they are composed, on the supposition that Mark did not exist at the time that Luke used Matthew in the composition of his Gospel.[46] While Griesbach was convinced that Mark used both Luke and Matthew (as we have them), he seems never to have investigated the precise nature of their relationship. Nevertheless this relationship must be cleared up before we can deal with the relationship of Mark with Luke-and-Matthew together.

Our first operation will therefore be to compare the unit sequence of Luke with that of Matthew, on the more likely assumption that Luke is subsequent to Matthew. The aim of the comparison is to discover if possible related patterns of units and topics.[47] For it is the particular arrangement of similar or identical idea-patterns that provides the strongest arguments for literary dependence; that is to say, if the 'bricks' or units of which the two documents are composed are seen to be built up partly in identical fashion and partly in intelligent divergence, there is no reasonable alternative to granting the indebtedness of the later editor to the earlier. In fact, if Luke is dependent on Matthew, we shall find that this fact will reveal itself more unmistakeably in the over-all pattern than in the interior structure of each unit.

§2 THE UNIT-SEQUENCE AGREEMENT OF LUKE WITH MATTHEW

The similarities between Matthew and Luke include a striking similarity of topics and a similarity of framework or main structure.[48] This is seen to good effect in Table I and Chart I where the respective units of Luke and Matthew have been applied to each other unit by unit.

This application reveals a remarkable sequential parallelism of units, which is emphasised by the horizontal parallel lines. These signify that all these units in Luke are in the same absolute and relative sequence as those in Matthew.[49] The exceptions are those where the lines are either diagonal or broken, in which case the parallels are mostly to be found in his Central section. There are less than twenty of the former transpositions and about fifty or more in the Central Section (the number varying according to different ways of reckoning).

Nearly all the units have a similar content but among them we have seen that there are some with the same topic but with a different content. Such are the Nativity narratives and the Resurrection narratives; such for example are the diverse Genealogies, the diverse accounts of the Nazareth Visits, the Calling of the Four Fishermen, and doublets such as the Parable of the Talents and the Parable of the Pounds.

It is of course true that within each individual unit there are also points of diversity as well as of similarity, and this is what we should expect from Luke's treatment of the units as a body. But generally speaking the units paralleled in the Greek synopses are linked precisely because scholars believe that their similarity is close enough to be fairly sure that they have at least a common source, even though each evangelist may have added original details from his private source.

The general parallelism of units is seen most clearly in Charts I and IIA, which have, as we said, been developed on the assumption that Luke knew and used Matthew, with Mark not yet thought of. It will however be noted that in a few places, and particularly at Lk 6:19, 7:1, 8:3 and 8:18, space has been left for Markan parallels with Matthew that in Luke are either omitted or transferred. These small gaps do not however diminish in any way the closeness of the Luke/Matthew relationship.

If we leave aside their respective Nativity and Resurrection narratives, we find that Matthew and Luke have some sixty-eight parallel units in absolute and relative sequences; another dozen in relative sequence only; and some fifty-four units that are parallel but in quite different sequence.[50] All in all, if we make allowance for the omission of doublets, or substitutions of similar material, and for the omission of material of local or ephemeral Palestinian interest, these (approximately) 134 units of Luke provide a more or less complete equivalent of the account of the ministry and teaching of Jesus as found in Matthew. And the top sixty-eight constitute a sort of basic common framework for the two Gospels. This massive agreement of Luke with Matthew may perhaps be grasped more clearly in another way, by describing the material according to topics, as in Table I which follows.

§3 TABLE I: SEQUENCE OF GOSPEL TOPICS

§	Chap: v.	MATTHEW	LUKE	Chap: v.
I	1, 2	Nativity Narrative	Nativity Narrative	1, 2
II	3:1;4:11	Preparation for Ministry	Preparation for Ministry	3:1–4:13
III	4:12-22	Jesus returns to Galilee	Jesus returns to Galilee; Nazareth Visit	4:14-43
IV	4:23 (8–9) (12:1-14) 4:24-25 (cf.12:15-16)	First Preaching Tour ——— ——— Gathering of Crowds, etc.	First Preaching Tour Miracles in Galilee Jesus & the Sabbath Gathering of Crowds, etc.	4:44 5:1-39 6:1-11 6:12-19
V	5–7	**The Great Sermon**	**The Great Sermon**	6:20-49
VI	8–9 8:5-13 ——— (11:2f) (13:1ff) (12:46-50) 8:23f; 9:18f	Miracles in Galilee The Centurion's Slave ——— ——— ——— ——— Three Miracles	——— The Centurion's Slave The Widow's Son Jesus & John, etc. **The Parables' Discourse** Anxiety of his Mother, etc. Three Miracles	(5:1–6:11) 7:1-10 7:11-17 7:18–8:3 8:4-18 8:19-21 8:22-56
VII	10:1-4 10:5-42 11:1 11:2-19 12:1-14 12:15f 12:46-50	Sending of Twelve & **Missionary Discourse** Journey continues Jesus & John, etc. Jesus & the Sabbath Jesus & Beelzebul etc. Anxiety of Mother,	Sending of Twelve & **Missionary Discourse** Journey continues ——— ——— ——— ———	9:1-2 9:3-5 9:6 (7:18-35) (6:1-11) (C/S) (8:19-21)
VIII	13:1-52	**Parables' Discourse**	———	(8:4-18)

§	Chap: v.	MATTHEW	LUKE	Chap: v.
IX	13:53f 14:1-2 14:13-21 14:22– 15:39 16:1– 17:27	Nazareth Visit Herod's Interest in Jesus Feeding of 5,000 Journey near Tyre & Sidon, etc. Peter's Confession, etc.	— Herod's Interest in Jesus Feeding of 5,000 — Peter's Confession etc.	(4:16-30) 9:7-9 9:10-17 — 9:18-45
X	18:1-35	Discourse on Forgiveness	Discourse on Forgiveness	9:46-48
XI	19:1 19:2– 21:21	Jesus leaves Galilee — The Judean Ministry	Jesus leave Galilee The Central Section The Judean Ministry	9:51 9:52– 18:14 18:15– 19:48
XII	21:22– 22:46	Disputations in Jerusalem	Disputations in Jerusalem	20:1-44
XIII	23:1-36 23:37-39	Denunciations of Scribes Lament over Jerusalem	Denunciations of Scribes The Widow's Mite	20:45-47 21:1-4
XIV	24, 25	Eschatological Discourse	Eschatological Discourse	21:5-36
XV	26, 27	Passion Narrative	Passion Narrative	22, 23
XVI	28	Resurrection Narrative	Resurrection Narrative	24

§4 EXPLANATION OF TABLE I

This table does not show all the minor divergencies of Luke's unit-sequence from Matthew's; these are found elsewhere in Chart I and in Volume II, *The Fourfold Gospel Synopsis*. It is simply meant to emphasise the main similarities and dissimilarities from the point of view of topics. The following comments are offered on this Table.

I. The Nativity Narratives

Both Matthew and Luke put this topic in the first place. It is of course true that their actual contents are diverse, but the topics are identical, and we are here dealing only with the over-all pattern.[51]

II. Preparation for the Ministry

Here the grouping of units is clear, including the fact that there are special Lukan additions that fit neatly into the Matthean narrative, e.g. Lk 3:1-2, 10-14. It is to be noted that the story of John the Baptist is narrated in the same sequence (not so in Mark), and that Lk 3:4-6 completes Matthew's quotation from Isaiah 40. Both Matthew and Luke provide Jesus with a long genealogy: but whereas Matthew starts from Abraham in order to show Jesus as the fulfilment of God's Promise to the Chosen People, Luke starts from Joseph, his legal father, and works his way back to Adam, the ancestor of Jew and Gentile, by another route. (This argues that Matthew is writing for Jewish Christians, and Luke for Gentile Christians.) It is worth noting that Luke's placing of his genealogy — at the end of the period of preparation — is not only entirely appropriate, but is an illustration of his making sure that his units on the same topic but with different content are never in the same sequence as their Matthean counterpart, cf. Lk 4:16ff; 10:25ff.

III. Jesus returns to Galilee

Luke and Matthew both begin with a short description of the first impact of Jesus' preaching, Mt 4:12-17 = Lk 4:14-15. Matthew then relates the Call of the Four Fishermen, which Luke transfers to the beginning of the First Preaching Tour, Mt 4:18-22 and Lk 5:1-11.

IV. The First Preaching Tour, Mt 4:23 = Lk 4:44

Whereas Matthew merely mentions this as a prelude to his description of the Gathering of the Crowds (Mt 4:24-25), Luke fills out this Tour with material which is found later in Matthew, in his chapters 8, 9 and 12. As Griesbach has pointed out (*Opusc. Acad. XXII*, p. 372 n.2, ed. Gabler, 1825), Luke has seen the connection between Mt 12:14-16 and 4:24-25 and decides to align his own Great Sermon at this point with a description of the Choosing of the Twelve and a list of their names (Lk 6:12-19).

V. The Great Sermon

Despite a number of important differences there can be no doubt that Luke's Sermon on the Plain is in essence the same as Matthew's Sermon on the Mount (see Chart IIA). Each has the same beginning, middle and ending, though Luke's is much shorter and has only Four Beatitudes with Four Woes, which are the converse of some of the Beatitudes. Hence its best common designation is the Great Sermon.

VI. Miracles in Galilee

In Matthew we now come to the long miracle section Mt 8:1–9:38, which aims to demonstrate that Jesus can act as well as speak with power and authority; but as Luke has already anticipated the use of much of this section, he is in sequence with Matthew here only with the unit of The Centurion's Slave. Luke however supplies a miracle from a special source — The Raising of the Widow's Son — intended to illustrate the units of John the Baptist material (Mt 11:2-19 = Lk 7:18-35) where Jesus refers to his raising of the dead. These Baptist units are in relative sequence with Matthew's, and the theme of the assault on the Kingdom forms in both Gospels the prelude to the Parables' Discourse, which Luke now relates (Lk 8:4-18), re-locating it before the 'three miracles' and the Missionary Discourse. Despite this shift of the Parables' Discourse, it is to be noted that Luke retains the identical sequence of Matthew for the three miracles of The Stilling of the Storm, the Gadarene Swine and the Raising of Jairus' Daughter. We note however that Luke reverses the relative position of The Anxiety of his Mother unit in relation to the Parables' Discourse, Lk 8:19-21 = Mt 12:46-50.

VII. Sending of the Twelve and the Missionary Discourse

Luke has now transferred all he intends to take from Mt 11 and 12 and comes back into parallel with Matthew for the Sending of the Twelve and the Missionary Discourse (or as much of it as he intends to leave in his main structure), and so arrives at

VIII. The Parables' Discourse in Matthew (13:1-50),

which Luke has already placed before his own Missionary Discourse at 8:4-18. He has now effected all his transfers except for some further transferences to the Central Section or to other Discourses: and so he comes back into parallel and absolute sequence with Matthew, as from Lk 9:7 (= Mt 14:1-2).

IX. Herod's Interest in Jesus and the latter part of the Galilean Ministry

Omitting Mt 13:53-58 (but see Lk 4:16-30), Luke, in sequence with Matthew, relates Herod's Interest in Jesus and the Feeding of the Five Thousand. He omits the Beheading of the Baptist, the Walking on the Water and the whole section Mt 14:22–15:39, sometimes known as The Great Lukan Omission. However he rejoins Matthew at 16:13 = Lk 9:18, with the Confession of Peter, the Transfiguration, the Healing of the Possessed Boy and the First Passion Prediction.

X. Discourse on Forgiveness (True Greatness)

This fourth Matthean Discourse again finds Luke in absolute sequence with Matthew, but again relating in his main framework only its beginning, other parts of it being found in The Central Section, Lk 17:1-4.

XI. Jesus leaves Galilee

At this point, Matthew describes Jesus as leaving Galilee for Judea and Transjordan, (Mt 19:1) and Luke similarly relates Jesus setting his face to go to Jerusalem, 9:51. At this same point however Luke inserts his 'Central Section' (9:52–18:14), which contains material drawn from every chapter of Mt 5–25, and notably from the Six Discourses, see Chart IIB. Luke, omitting Mt 19:3-12, rejoins Matthew at his 18:15, and thereafter relates in parallel sequence the journey up to Jerusalem.

XII-XVI. Jerusalem Material

In the remaining sections Luke has the identical sequence of Matthew, despite the occasional transfer or omission, e.g. Mt 27:3-10 (but cf. Acts 1:17-20); Mt 22:34-40 = Lk 10:25-28. Luke again gives in his main framework only the beginning of The Denunciation of the Pharisees and Scribes, and of the Eschatological Discourse repectively, the rest of what he takes of both being found in his Central Section. He also contrives a (seventh) Last Supper Discourse, which contains elements saved up from Matthean units that he has earlier passed over, see Lk 22:24-38; the over-all sequence however remains undisturbed. As to the Resurrection narratives, though they are for the most part diverse in content (and entirely so after Lk 24:12), yet both agree that the women were the first to learn from the angels of the disappearance of the Body of Jesus, and that Jesus subsequently appeared to the Eleven, though each gives a different location.

§5 A REVIEW OF TABLE I

This Table illustrates very well the way in which Luke adheres firmly to certain fixed points in Matthew's framework. What is especially clear is that in the very places where Luke's sequence varies from Matthew's (IV-VIII) there still remain a number of fixed points (the First Preaching Tour, the Gathering of the Crowds, the Great Sermon, the Centurion's Slave, the Sending of the Twelve, the Missionary Discourse, Herod's Interest in Jesus) where their joint sequence remains absolutely the same. Thus the units which Luke re-groups in his own way in chapters 4–8 are still grouped round the same fixed points. Moreover Luke retains every one of Matthew's topics, except for those in his Great Omission. The quality and amount of agreement is in fact so high as strongly to urge assent to the conclusion that the one Gospel must be in some real literary dependence on the other, i.e. that Luke has adopted the actual pattern and sequence of Matthew, with the reservations stated.

However this Table highlights not only their similarities but also their dissimilarities. For it reveals the transference of basically Matthean material to the place in Luke where it helps to illustrate and fill out the First Preaching Tour, to which Matthew only refers in passing; it reveals the 'switch' of the Parables' Discourse together with the materials adjoining it, e.g. The Anxiety of Mother and Brethren unit. It also reveals the so-called Great Lukan Omission, opposite to Mt 14:22–15:39. And finally, it reveals the skilful insertion of the Central Section at the head of the material concerned with the Judean Ministry at a point after Mt 19:1. These are some of the phenomena that any sound theory of Luke's use of Matthew must also convincingly explain. We may now turn to these dissimilarities in detail.

CHAPTER SEVEN

THE DISSIMILARITIES

§1 SUMMARY OF THE DISSIMILARITIES AS REGARDS UNIT-SEQUENCE

These dissimilarities may be classified under the following heads, as different types of sequential displacement:

1) *a single alteration* to the main common structure, namely the switch of position of the Parables' Discourse; and
   a single addition to the main structure of Luke by the insertion of his Central Section (Lk 9:52–18:14). It is to be noted that the Journey Section of Luke (9:51–19:28) has two distinct parts, consisting of the Central Section (which is also cast in the form of a journey) and the Journey narrative common to all three Synoptic Gospels. For after the linking verse Lk 9:51 = Mt 19:1, there follows the Central Section, which on closer inspection will be found to be a specially created literary device of Luke containing a careful selection of Gospel teaching material; and only after this does that part of Luke's Journey Section begin (18:15–19:28), which runs parallel to the Journey Sections of Matthew and Mark (Mt 19 and 20 = Mk 10). In other words the Central Section is a unit on its own and prefaces the common journey account that Luke shares with Matthew and Mark.
2) the transfer (or displacement) of certain story-units between Mt 4 and 13 to a new place and sequence between Lk 4 and 8, in every case within their common structure.
3) the transfer (or displacement) to Luke's Central Section (9:52–18:14) of a large number of units found between Mt 5 and 25. See Chart IIB.
4) Lukan additions to Matthew.
5) Lukan omissions of Matthean units.

These categories cover all the main differences between the Lukan and Matthean pattern. The following detailed description is offered for each.

47

§2 THE SWITCH OF POSITION OF THE PARABLES' DISCOURSE

The following units are involved:

Preaching in Parables	Mt 13:1-2	Lk 8:4
Parable of the Sower	Mt 13:3-9	Lk 8:5-8
Reason for Using Parables	Mt 13:10-15	Lk 8:9-10
Explanation of 'The Sower'	Mt 13:18-23	Lk 8:11-15

It will be noted that the Lukan parallels are found transferred in the same relative sequence to another place in Luke's framework (see also Chart I). Note too that the four units are displaced *en bloc*; (though missing from Luke in the course of the transfer is the Matthean Sayings-unit 'Blessed your eyes', Mt 13:16-17, which is found paralleled in Luke at 10:23-24 in his Central Section). The net effect of this move is to put these four units *before* the Lukan Missionary Discourse (Lk 9:1-6 = Mt 10:5ff). Yet this switch has been effected without otherwise spoiling either the exact parallelism of the main structure of the two Gospels or the identical sequence of the other four Discourses, thus:

Mt 5–7	Sermon on the Mount	—	Sermon on the Plain	Lk 6:20-49
			Parables' Discourse	Lk 8:5-16
Mt 10:1f	Missionary Discourse	—	Missionary Discourse	Lk 9:1-6
Mt 13:1f	Parables' Discourse			
Mt 18:1f	Discourse on Community		Discourse on Community	Lk 9:46-48
Mt 23:1f	Denunciation of Scribes	—	Denunciation of Scribes	Lk 20:45-47
Mt 24:1f	Eschatological Discourse	—	Eschatological Discourse	Lk 21:5-36

This is the only alteration that Luke makes when adopting the *framework* of Matthew. As to the Central Section (Lk 9:52–18:14), this is a skilful addition, achieved by placing it within the Journey to Jerusalem Section, thus making Lk 9:51 + (9:52–18:14) + 18:15–19:28 = Mt 19:1–20:34. In conseqence, the Central Section, which occupies nearly one third of the total length of Luke, in no way spoils either the parallelism or the sequence of the Matthean-Lukan framework.

§3 THE TRANSFER OF UNITS FOUND IN LUKE 4–8

i.e. Lukan story-units parallel to Matthew, that are found transferred to other places within Luke's modified version of the Matthean structure, see §1, 2)

We are concerned here with the story-units between Mt 4 and 13 that are found paralleled in Luke 4–8. What has happened to the sequence of these units can be seen in Chart I.

1) We take first of all three units having the same general topic, but different content:

Luke's Genealogy of Jesus, which is quite different in content from Matthew's and which is found immediately after the Baptism of Jesus at Lk 3:23-38, on the threshold of Jesus' Public Ministry.

The Nazareth Visit of Mt 13:53-58, which is transferred by Luke out of sequence to Lk 4:16-30, the content of which has very little in common with Matthew's.

The Call of Four Fishermen (Lk 5:1-11) has only one sentence in common with Matthew's account, 4:18-22, and is in fact out of sequence with Matthew.

Thus the peculiarity of all three of the above units is that though they refer respectively to the same topic, place and event, their actual content is not similar for the most part and they are found in Luke out of sequence with their Matthean counterpart. We may now note that whenever he has a unit with the same topic as a corresponding Matthean unit but with a different content, Luke never places it in the same absolute or relative sequence with its Matthean counterpart, but always in another context. Thus the Genealogy is placed last after Jesus' Baptism, at the end of the period of Preparation, instead of first as in Matthew. The Call of the Four Fishermen is also re-sited, but still retains its sequence as taking place prior to the Preaching Tour. The place of the Nazareth Visit in Luke seems to be due to a Lukan tradition which records a rejection of Jesus by his own native city at the very beginning of his public life. The new location avoids a clash with the different story told in Mt 13:53ff, and also provides Luke with the ideal dramatic introduction to the Ministry of Jesus by means of his quotation of Isaiah 60:1ff.

Another example is found at Lk 10:25-28 (= Mt 22:34-40), in the Central Section.

2) The next group consists of six units which are out of sequence with Matthew, but which are yet certainly parallel and similar in content. They are:

The Cleansing of a Leper (Mt 8:1-4 = Lk 5:12-16). Whereas in Matthew this is the first miracle after the Sermon on the Mount and illustrates Jesus' respect for the authority of the Mosaic Priesthood, in Luke it becomes the first story-unit of the First Preaching Tour of Galilee

(Lk 4:44–6:11). Hence although it loses its sequence relative to the other story-units transferred (see 3) below) it still remains the first Lukan miracle story of this First Preaching Tour.

The Plucking of Grain on the Sabbath (Mt 12:1-8 = Lk 6:1-5) and *The Healing of the Man with a Withered Hand on the Sabbath* (Mt 12:9-14 = Lk 6:6-11) may be taken together as they are transferred together. In Matthew these two story-units are used to prepare the reader for the hostility to Jesus described in Mt 12:17-37; Luke on the other hand, takes them out of the Matthean sequence and places them at the climax of the First Preaching Tour. Hence in Luke the Cleansing of a Leper and these two stories are respectively placed first and last in the series of events which precede his Sermon on the Plain, just as in their Matthean context (between the Great Sermon and the Suffering Servant theme), they are here also the first and last of their series.[52]

The Anxiety of Jesus' Mother and Brothers (Lk 8:19-21) is the fourth of this group.

Here Luke sets it in a sequence slightly different from Matthew's, putting it after the Parables' Discourse, while in Matthew it comes immediately before. It is not easy to assign the reason for this slight deviation on the part of Luke, but we may note for future reference that Mark returns it to the Matthean (relative) sequence.

Lastly we have a double unit, The Choice of the Twelve and The Names of the Twelve.

The Choice of the Twelve, Mt 5:1 = Lk 6:12-13 (= Mk 3:13). There seems to be little doubt that these texts are in exact parallel; for the conjunction of the Great Crowds, Mt 4:24-25 = Lk 6:17-19 (= Mk 3:7-12), with Jesus ascending the mountain, praying there (Mt and Lk only), and then calling the disciples to himself, must be more than a random coincidence. It is to be noted that Matthew 5:1 only hints at the process of selection which Luke unfolds. This is of course in line with Luke's pattern of developing seminal phrases of Matthew, the previous example being his unfolding of Mt 4:23.

As regards *The Names of the Twelve*, Mt 10:2-4 = Lk 6:14-16 (= Mk 3:16b-19), Luke transfers the list in such a way as to retain almost but not quite the same relative sequence as Matthew (see 3) below). In Matthew this unit is found attached quite naturally to the Commissioning of the Twelve, whereas Luke attaches it to their Choosing, which Matthew does not describe in detail. Luke puts it before the unit describing the Great Gathering of Crowds. (Again we may note that Mark restores this unit also to the same relative sequence as it has in Matthew, viz. after the Gathering of the Crowds.)

3) The remaining seven units are found transferred in Luke in such a way as to retain the same relative sequence to one another (and also in fact to the transferred Parables unit, already dealt with).

The Healing of Peter's Mother-in-law (Mt 8:14-15 = Lk 4:38-39) and *Many Healings outside the House* (Mt 8:16-17 = Luke 4:40-41) go together. Here Luke's motive for transfer would seem to be chronological;[53] for he separates these two items from the other miracle stories he transfers (cf. Lk 5:12–6:11), because they describe events which occurred at the place from which Jesus began the Preaching Tour that led to the Great Sermon, i.e. at Peter's house.

The Healing of a Paralytic (Mt 9:1-8 = Lk 5:17-26), *The Call of Matthew (Levi)* (Mt 9:9-13 = Lk 5:27-32), and *A Question about Fasting* (Mt 9:14-17 = Lk 5:33-39) are found transferred by Luke as if they were a single unit and are delicately inserted between The Cleansing of a Leper and the two 'Sabbath Infringement' units, just described above. These five units together with The Cleansing of the Leper (5:12-16) comprise all that Luke tells us of the period of the First Tour of Galilee, i.e. between Jesus' departure from Capharnaum (Lk 4:44) and The Choosing of the Twelve (Lk 6:12), just before the Sermon on the Plain. Three of them in fact describe events that took place in Capharnaum itself, but the others indicate another location.[54]

The final two units transferred in the same relative sequence as Matthew's, are attached by Luke to the period between the Great Sermon and the Parables' Discourse, namely *John's Envoys* and *Jesus' Praise of John* (Mt 11:2-19 = Lk 7:18-35). This seems to be the right place chronologically speaking. For it was the great fame of Jesus which came to its climax at the Great Sermon that reached John and caused him to send his envoys to question Jesus.

4) Remaining displacements in Luke 4–8.

As regards the events after the Great Sermon, Luke has decided that everything else that he wants out of Mt 8–12 and 13 (except for Central Section transfers), is best re-arranged to fit in between the Sermon and the Missionary Discourse. Luke considers that the two units about John the Baptist (Mt 11:2-19 = Lk 7:18-35) belong to this period and brings them forward accordingly. The introduction into this section of *The Raising of the Widow's Son at Naim* unit seems to have been prompted by Jesus' instructions to the disciples of John to tell their master that 'the dead are being raised' (Lk 7:22). The next unit, *The Sinful Woman's Anointing of Jesus*, is certainly intended to show that even the most despised and abandoned class of sinners may come to Jesus with confidence and hope, Lk 7:36-50. This is followed by a description of Jesus' entourage not found elsewhere, 8:1-3. Luke then introduces the Parables' Discourse, the only Discourse of Matthew of which he changes the position, and then proceeds to pick up in order the other units he has passed over until he comes to the Missionary Discourse.

§4 MATTHEAN UNITS TRANSFERRED BY LUKE TO HIS CENTRAL SECTION

These fall into two categories; those coming from the Six Discourses, and those coming from the intervening chapters, see Chart IIB.

1) *Transfers from the Six Discourses,* i.e. from Mt 5—7, 10, 13, 18, 23 and 25. We here bring to light two facts hitherto unnoticed: firstly, there is a sequential parallel to the first part of each Matthean Discourse to be found in Luke's main structure in Luke's shortened form of it, i.e. Lk 6:20-22 = Mt 5:2-11; Lk 8:4-18 = Mt 13:1-15, 18-23; Lk 9:1-6 = Mt 10:1-15; Lk 9:46-48 = Mt 18:1-2, 4-5; Lk 20:45-47 = Mt 23:1-13; Lk 21:5-33 = Mt 24:4-36; secondly, Luke transfers to his Central Section the rest of the material that he takes out of these six Discourses, except for a few Sayings units which he joins on to his abbreviated versions of these Discourses in his main structure.[55]

In other words, each Discourse as an event is represented recognisably in Luke's main structure, but the rest of what he takes from each is found in the appropriate area of his Central Section (save for exceptions in note 55). Moreover, while Luke preserves the Matthean sequence of the Discourses (except for the switch of the Parables' Discourse) and also preserves the sequence of Matthean material in his shortened versions of these Discourses, *the sequence of the material transferred to the Central Section bears no direct relation at all to its sequence in Matthew.* This discriminating practice of Luke is the ground for the diverse treatment given to the Central Section material in Chart I, IIA & IIB. (Luke's practice is well demonstrated by his treatment of the Great Sermon, see Chart IIA, and Excursus on Luke's Adaptation of the Great Sermon, *Chapter Eight,* §4 below.)

2) *The remaining transfers to the Central Section* are taken from the chapters intervening between the Six Discourses, namely, Mt 8—9, 11—12, 14—17, 19—22, see Chart IIB. But here Luke does not do what he did with the Discourses, i.e. divide the material into two categories, leaving one part *in situ* and transferring the rest; on the contrary, when he takes a unit from these chapters, he takes the whole of it, does not re-locate it in another part of the main structure, but transfers it straight into the Central Section. See Excursus on the Central Section for further detail, *Chapter Eight,* §3 below.

This discriminating practice of Luke is the key to his seemingly extraordinary action in shredding the Discourses of Matthew and dispersing the material. Whatever his intention may have been, what he did in fact was to separate the main outline and structure of the life of Jesus from his Message and Teachings; and he establishes this teaching section without disturbing his main framework. In this framework he mostly follows the sequence of Matthew, but he gathers up Jesus' Teachings quite otherwise. These re-arrangements of Luke properly explain what many have thought to be a jumble of clueless transpositions and show his Gospel to be a purposeful re-editing.

§5 LUKAN ADDITIONS TO MATTHEW

Luke introduces a considerable number of new units, reminiscences, parables and other teachings, most of which occur in the Central Section. See Chart IIB, where the new units are marked with an asterisk. he also introduces a few new units into his main structure, e.g. 4:33-37; 7:11-17; 9:49-50; 21:1-4; 22:24-38 (where he greatly augments Matthew's Last Supper Discourse); 23:6-12.

In a number of cases Luke offers a doublet of a Matthean unit, i.e. substitutes either his own version or a similar story; such units are sufficiently diverse for him to re-locate them in another non-Matthean sequence, e.g. he substitutes his own Great Supper Parable for Matthew's Royal Feast, his own Parable of the Pounds for Matthew's Parable of the Talents, his own anointing story for Matthew's (Lk 7:36-50, Mt 26:6f); his own fig-tree story in place of Matthew's (Lk 13:6f, Mt 21:9f); and none are in sequence with their Matthean counterpart.

§6 LUKAN OMISSIONS OF MATTHEAN UNITS

These consist of:

1) Omitting Matthew's version of certain units and substituting his own, see under §5 above;
2) Omission of Matthean Doublets, e.g. Luke omits Matthew's Feeding of the Four Thousand, having already given (along with Matthew) the Five Thousand; he also omits the Matthean story of the death of John the Baptist, as he has spoken of his imprisonment earlier at Lk 3:19-20; also some Parables of the Kingdom and some Parables of Watchfulness.
3) Units of the so-called Great Omission.[56] N.B. As we are dealing solely with the units that compose the Gospels, the Lukan omissions of items from within individual units, e.g. the omission of Mt 11:28-30 and 16:17-19, do not come up for consideration here.

CHAPTER EIGHT

SOME EXAMPLES OF THE LUKE-MATTHEW RELATIONSHIP

In this Chapter we shall take four examples as illustrations of Luke's editorial work on Matthew:

§1 The Centurion's Slave Unit, Mt 8:5-13 = Lk 7:1-10
§2 The First Preaching Tour in Galilee, Lk 4:44–6:19
§3 The Central Section, Lk 9:51–18:14
§4 The Great Sermon
§5 A Provisional Conclusion

§1 THE CENTURION'S SLAVE (Mt 8:5-13 = Lk 7:1-10)

It happens that the Centurion's Slave unit is the only story unit common to Luke and Matthew that has no Markan parallel. Hence it is possible to test the conclusions of this chapter upon it without risk of confusion or suspicion of Markan influence.

The Centurion's Slave *(BO 91)*

Mt 8:5-13	Lk 7:1-10
(cf. 7:28ᵃ)	¹ Ἐπειδὴ ἐπλήρωσεν πάντα τὰ ῥήματα αὐτοῦ εἰς τὰς ἀκοὰς τοῦ λαοῦ,
⁵ Εἰσελθόντες δέ αὐτοῦ εἰς Καφαρναοὺμ προςῆλθεν αὐτῷ ἑκατόνταρχος παρακαλῶν αὐτὸν ⁶ καὶ λέγων· κύριε, ὁ παῖς μου βέβληται ἐν τῇ οἰκίᾳ παραλυτικός, δεινῶς βασανιζόμενος.	εἰσῆλθεν εἰς Καφαρναούμ. ² Ἑκατοντάρχου δέ τινος δοῦλος κακῶς ἔχων

Mt 8:5-13	Lk 7:1-10
	ἤμελλεν τελευτᾶν, ὃς ἦν αὐτῷ ἔντιμος.
	³ ἀκούσας δὲ περὶ τοῦ Ἰησοῦ ἀπέστειλεν πρὸς αὐτὸν πρεσβυτέρους τῶν Ἰουδαίων ἐρωτῶν αὐτὸν ὅπως ἐλθὼν διασώσῃ τὸν δοῦλον αὐτοῦ.
	⁴ οἱ δὲ παραγενόμενοι πρὸς τὸν Ἰησοῦν παρεκάλουν αὐτὸν σπουδαίως, λέγοντες ὅτι ἄξιός ἐστιν ᾧ παρέξῃ τοῦτο·
	⁵ ἀγαπᾷ γὰρ τὸ ἔθνος ἡμῶν καὶ τὴν συναγωγὴν αὐτὸς ᾠκοδόμησεν ἡμῖν.
⁷ καὶ λέγει αὐτόν· ἐγὼ ἐλθὼν θεραπεύσω αὐτόν.	⁶ ὁ δέ Ἰησοῦς ἐπορεύετο σὺν αὐτοῖς.
	ἤδη δέ αὐτοῦ οὐ μακρὰν ἀπέχοντος ἀπὸ τῆς οἰκίας, ἔπεμψεν φίλους
⁸ καὶ ἀποκριθεὶς ὁ ἑκατόνταρχος ἔφη·	ὁ ἑκατοντάρχης λέγων αὐτῷ·
κύριε,	κύριε, μὴ σκύλλου·
οὐκ εἰμὶ ἱκανὸς ἵνα μου ὑπὸ τὴν στέγην εἰσέλθῃς·	οὐ γὰρ ἱκανός εἰμι ἵνα ὑπὸ τὴν στέγην μου εἰσέλθῃς·
	⁷ διὸ οὐδὲ ἐμαυτὸν ἠξίωσα πρὸς σὲ ἐλθεῖν·
ἀλλὰ μόνον εἰπὲ λόγῳ, καὶ ἰαθήσεται ὁ παῖς μου.	ἀλλὰ εἰπὲ λόγῳ, καὶ ἰαθήτω ὁ παῖς μου.
⁹ καὶ γὰρ ἐγὼ ἄνθρωπός εἰμι ὑπὸ ἐξουσίαν, ἔχων ὑπ' ἐμαυτὸν στρατιώτας, καὶ λέγω τούτῳ· πορεύθητι, καὶ πορεύεται, καὶ ἄλλῳ· ἔρχου, καὶ ἔρχεται, καὶ τῷ δούλῳ μου· ποίησον τοῦτο, καὶ ποιεῖ.	⁸ καὶ γὰρ ἐγὼ ἄνθρωπός εἰμι ὑπὸ ἐξουσίαν τασσόμενος, ἔχων ὑπ' ἐμαυτὸν στρατιώτας, καὶ λέγω τούτῳ· πορεύθητι, καὶ πορεύεται, καὶ ἄλλῳ· ἔρχου, καὶ ἔρχεται, καὶ τῷ δούλῳ μου· ποίησον τοῦτο, καὶ ποιεῖ.
¹⁰ ἀκούσας δέ ὁ Ἰησοῦς ἐθαύμασεν καὶ	⁹ ἀκούσας δέ ταῦτα ὁ Ἰησοῦς ἐθαύμασεν αὐτόν, καὶ στραφεὶς τῷ ἀκολουθοῦντι αὐτῷ ὄχλῳ εἶπεν·
εἶπεν τοῖς ἀκολουθοῦσιν· Ἀμὴν, λέγω ὑμῖν, παρ' οὐδενὶ τοσαύτην πίστιν ἐν τῷ	λέγω ὑμῖν, οὐδὲ ἐν τῷ Ἰσραὴλ τοσαύτην πίστιν

Mt 8:5-13	Lk 7:1-10
Ἰσραὴλ εὗρον. ¹¹ λέγω δὲ ὑμῖν ὅτι πολλοὶ ἀπὸ ἀνατολῶν καὶ δυσμῶν ἥξουσιν, καὶ ἀνακλιθήσονται μετὰ Ἀβραὰμ καὶ Ἰσαὰκ καὶ Ἰακὼβ ἐν τῇ βασιλείᾳ τῶν οὐρανῶν· ¹² οἱ δὲ υἱοὶ τῆς βασιλείας ἐκβληθήσονται εἰς τὸ σκότος τὸ ἐξώτερον· ἐκεῖ ἔσται ὁ κλαυθμὸς καὶ ὁ βρυγμὸς τῶν ὀδόντων. ¹³ καὶ εἶπεν ὁ Ἰησοῦς τῷ ἑκατοντάρχῃ· ὕπαγε, ὡς ἐπίστευσας γενηθήτω σοι. καὶ ἰάθη ὁ παῖς αὐτοῦ ἐν τῇ ὥρᾳ ἐκείνῃ.	εὗρον. cf. 13:28-29 ¹⁰ καὶ ὑποστρέψαντες εἰς τὸν οἶκον οἱ πεμφθέντες εὗρον τὸν δοῦλον ὑγιαίνοντα.

These are some of the noteworthy features that emerge from the comparison:

1) As regards the situation of this unit in the respective Gospels: Matthew makes it the second healing after the Great Sermon, his first being the Cure of a Leper with the instruction to go and fulfil the requirements of the Mosaic Law, cf. Mt 8:1-4 and 5:15f.

Luke however makes it his first healing after the Great Sermon, because he has already transferred the Healing of the Leper to Lk 5:12f in order to make it the first cure of Jesus' First Preaching Tour. Hence Luke is in fact faithful to the intention of Matthew, while also here emphasising the important place of the Gentiles in the Kingdom of God.

2) There is a great contrast between the close verbal agreement in the dialogue and the variations of expression in the narrative portions of the unit.

3) In Matthew the Centurion would appear to come to Jesus in person, whereas in Luke he first sends elders and later friends, but never himself comes in Jesus' presence.

4) Luke alone gives the true reason why the Centurion utters the 'Lord, I am not worthy, etc.'; for on learning that Jesus has agreed to come to his house, he is suddenly so overwhelmed by his own unworthiness that he sends a message that Jesus need only say the word from

wherever he happens to be.

5) Luke in fact has an expanded version of the narrative portions of the story, without however omitting a single item of Matthew's account. His additional details dovetail neatly into Matthew's version, e.g. Lk 7:2-5 with Mat 8:6-7. Matthew gives the barest minimum necessary to show Jesus' power. Luke not only has all that Matthew has, but adds much more without however contradicting him.

6) Luke reads exactly like an expansion of Matthew by one who has many more details in his own source. It would be extremely difficult to reduce Luke to Matthew; for to remove the intervention of the Centurion's friends would be greatly to impoverish the story. Whereas if Matthew was the original *chreia*, Luke is easily seen as a natural expansion by means of another source, combined with Luke's own editorial activity upon Matthew.

7) Mt 8:11-12, in which Jesus foretells the exclusion of the sons of the Kingdom, looks like a Matthean editorial addition to the original story. Indeed Luke has understood it in this sense, and has removed it to his Central Section to the place where someone said to Jesus, 'Lord, will those who are saved be few?', Lk 13:28-29.

8) It is unlikely that the two versions come from one report. Certainly Matthew does not come from Luke.

9) The evidence of the use of παῖς and δοῦλος in this unit supports Luke's dependence on Matthew. For παῖς is the 'vulgar' word for slave, though in another context it can equally mean 'son'; Matthew uses it in the former sense throughout this passage. Not so Luke, who uses παῖς here only once when quoting the words of the Centurion. In the other sentences at the beginning and the end he uses δοῦλος, slave, to show that the person concerned is not the Centurion's son, but his slave. Luke is here clearly interpreting Matthew's παῖς and not *vice versa*. In other words, this usage argues decisively for Luke's knowledge of Matthew.

10) Further proof that Luke is the borrower comes from Mt 8:8-10 = Lk 7:6c-9. For the additions to the Matthean text found in this passage where the two texts are all but identical (namely, διὸ οὐδὲ ἐμαυτὸν ἠξίωσα πρὸς σὲ ἐλθεῖν, τασσόμενος, ταῦτα, στραφεὶς τῷ, αὐτῷ ὄχλῳ), are 'just the unnecessary exegetical additions which Luke loves' (Chapman, *Matthew, Mark and Luke*, p. 103).[57]

To sum up, Luke's editorial procedure in this passage is a replica in miniature of what we have seen him doing with the Gospel units in relation to the whole Gospel. For (a) he adds important and illuminating detail which invariably fits inside the Matthean pattern and which gives a new dimension to the story, (b) he removes an item slanted against the Jews (here it is Mt 8:11-12, about their exclusion from the Kingdom, as being alien to the unit itself, though in fact one of Matthew's important themes). Nevertheless, (c) he transfers this item to his Central Section, to a part dealing with Entrance into the Kingdom. (d) In the main, he follows Matthew.

§2 THE FIRST PREACHING TOUR, Luke 4:44–6:19

If we now pause a moment to look at what Luke has done here, we suddenly realise the rationality of his procedure. All these Lukan changes have one main object, namely the sorting out of the material in Matthew 4–12 to enable Luke to give shape to Jesus' First Preaching Tour in Galilee, which started from Peter's house and ended at the Great Sermon. What he does is to single out some eight units and cause them to converge within this period. Chart I shows this diagramatically.

In the first place, Luke decided to retain the same absolute and relative order as Matthew with regard to some sixty-eight units, of which some twenty-one are in his first thirteen chapters. In the next place, he decided to expand Matthew's very brief mention of the First Preaching Tour (Mt 4:23) into a more lengthy account (Lk 4:44–6:16). He begins by transferring his own account of the Call of the Four Fishermen so as to inform the reader that these four were with Jesus from the beginning of this tour (Lk 5:1-11), and that they were in fact the first four to be called. (No doubt this is connected with the later importance in the Church of Peter, James and John.) He then selects Matthew's first post-Sermon miracle, the Cleansing of the Leper (Mt 9:1-4), and makes it the first miracle of this tour, (Lk 5:12-16). In Matthew it was clearly put first because it was meant to re-affirm the words of Jesus in the Great Sermon that he had come to fulfil, and not to destroy, the Law of Moses; for in both Matthean and Lukan accounts Jesus tells the leper to 'go, show yourself to the priest, and offer the gift that Moses commanded, as a proof to the people'. A further reason is to demonstrate that Jesus the Messiah shows his favour first to a representative of his own people by working a miracle on him. This was why Matthew put this miracle first after the Great Sermon, and Luke succeeds in preserving the objective of Matthew by making the same miracle the first of the First Preaching Tour.

The second miracle of Matthew's post-Sermon section is the Healing of the Centurion's Slave (Mt 8:5-13), which Luke passes over at this moment because he has already decided to retain it in the original Matthean order, merely moving it up to become the first recorded miracle of Jesus after the Sermon on the Plain. For Luke had noted its suitablity for this purpose, namely to stand as the first beneficent act of Jesus towards a Gentile, a sign of the grace and healing now being made available in equal measure to the Gentiles.

Next on the list for transfer come the incidents connected with Peter's house (Mt 8:14-17). Their significance for Matthew was not so much that the third of his miracles is directed to a relative of Peter as it was a sign that Jesus' mission is 'to take on our infirmities and bear our diseases' (Isaiah 53:4). But Luke transfers this unit (while dropping out on the way the reference to Isaiah) to a position prior to the First Preaching Tour, his aim seeming to be the practical one of letting us know that it was from Peter's house in Capharnaum that Jesus really began his apostolic ministry in Galilee.

The next unit in Matthew (8:18-22) is scheduled for transfer out of the main story into the Central Section. Its place in Matthew was due to the editor's desire to inform the reader that Jesus' disciples have to share his homelessness and complete detachment. Luke considers that it will be better placed in that early part of the Central Section devoted to the question of discipleship (Lk 9:57-60).

Luke passes over the next two units (the Stilling of the Storm and the Gadarene Swine, Mt 8:23-34) as he has previously decided to leave them in the same absolute and relative order as in Matthew (see Chart I). And this brings him to three units (the Paralytic, the Call of Levi and the Question of the Sabbath, Mt 9:1-8, 9-13, 14-17) which he has decided to transfer as a consecutive group in order to build up the content of the First Preaching Tour. As in Matthew, they illustrate Jesus' authority to forgive sins, his will to call 'sinners, not the righteous', and the impossibility of his new teaching fitting in with the 'old wineskins' of the Mosaic regulations.

And finally to conclude the material he wished to incorporate into the Tour, Luke passes over the rest of Matthew 9, 10 and 11 and transfers the two units relating to his teaching about the Sabbath, namely, the Plucking of the Grain and the Healing of the Man with a Withered Hand, Mt 12:1-8, 9-15 = Lk 6:1-5, 6-11. It is to be noted that from this point, 12:16, onwards to the end of the chapter, Matthew records the ferment created in the minds of the Scribes and Pharisees by all these new teachings and miracles of Jesus together with his rebukes and warnings, almost all of which Luke has transferred to his Central Section.

Returning to the two Sabbath units, we see that Luke uses them to form the climax of the First Preaching Tour just as they form a climax in Matthew in another sequence. They are followed by Jesus' withdrawal and subsequent Choice of the Twelve after a night spent in prayer, 6:12-13, and Luke tidily and efficiently transfers the list of the names of the Twelve to this point also, 6:14-16. Luke then skips back from Mt 12:15-16 to Mt 4:24-25, which is exactly parallel to his own 6:17-19, both recording the circumstances that lead to the Great Sermon, Lk 6: 20-49 = Mt 5–7.

§3 EXCURSUS ON THE CENTRAL SECTION OF LUKE (9:52–18:14)

There is as yet no satisfactory study of the Central Section. In the bibliography appended to this Excursus are given some recent major contributions in the form of articles known to the writer. The article of Professor Reicke is the one that comes nearest to grasping its true function in the economy of Luke's Gospel. But none of them have fully understood that it is basically a literary device to set apart, to illustrate and to develop, the teaching of Jesus as unfolded principally in the six Discourses of St Matthew's Gospel. While Matthew preserves the teaching of Jesus in a series of great Discourses, Luke achieves the same object in a more sophisticated manner by means of his Central Section. This is the reason for his first dismembering and then putting together again the Sayings of Jesus as found in Matthew. And this editorial procedure was forced upon him because of the requirements he set himself, namely:

1) to respect the pattern and content of the First Gospel,
2) to re-interpret the Gospel Message in language that would make sense to the Gentile Christians of Paul's churches,
3) to make room for the inclusion of many new stories about Jesus and for the addition of much new detail regarding other stories already known to the Church.

The following notes may help to provide some of the lines along which future research must proceeed.

Firstly, the material parallel to Matthew is carefully interspersed with special Lukan material, viz:
Lk 9:52-56, 10:1-12, 10:17-20, 10:29-42, 11:5-8, 12:13-21, 13:1-17, 13:31-33, 14:1-24, 15:8–16:12, 16:14-15, 16:19-31, 17:7-21, 18:1-13.

Secondly, the Lukan Sayings Doublets will certainly repay further study; for one member of each of these doublets is found in the Central Section and the other member in the main structure, namely:

Lk 8:16 =	Lk 11:33
8:17 =	12:2
9:24 =	17:33
9:26 =	12:9
9:50 =	11:23
20:46 =	11:43

The exceptions are Lk 8:8:18 = 19:26, where the second member is found outside the Central Section, although within the common Journey Section, which actually ends at the following verse (19:27); and 14:11 = 18:14, where both members are found within the Central Section proper.

Thirdly, the method pursued by Luke in building up the Central Section deserves attention. The study of Chart IIB would suggest that after a preliminary attempt to interweave the Matthean Sayings with his new material, which proved too complicated, he adopted a prosaic 'rule of thumb'. For after eliminating in advance all the Matthean material he intended to exclude from his Gospel, he is seen to move steadily forward time after time through the material he intended to retain until he had exhausted it.

For example, as regards Mt 13 (partly paralleled in Lk 8:4-5), we find him taking up the following pieces of Mt 13 in the order in which they are found in Matthew, the theme being participation in the Kingdom, i.e.

$$\begin{aligned} \text{Mt } 13{:}16\text{-}17 &= \text{Lk } 10{:}23\text{-}24 \\ 13{:}31\text{-}32 &= 13{:}18\text{-}19 \\ 13{:}33 &= 13{:}20\text{-}21 \end{aligned}$$

But his practice is most strikingly exemplified in the Great Sermon, where there is a much more complicated pattern of selection, i.e.:

Material on Prayer,

$$\begin{aligned} \text{Mt } 6{:}9\text{-}13 &= \text{Lk } 11{:}1\text{-}4 \\ 7{:}7\text{-}11 &= 11{:}9\text{-}13 \end{aligned}$$

and then Luke goes back again to near the beginning and starts to go through it again, on the subject of Inner Cleanliness, i.e.

$$\begin{aligned} \text{Mt } 5{:}15 &= \text{Lk } 11{:}33 \\ 6{:}22\text{-}23 &= 11{:}34\text{-}36 \end{aligned}$$

and on Detachment from Possessions, i.e.

$$\text{Mt } 6{:}25\text{-}34 = \text{Lk } 12{:}22\text{-}32$$

He then returns again for the next item, Treasure in Heaven,

$$\text{Mt } 6{:}19\text{-}21 = \text{Lk } 12{:}33\text{-}34$$

He then goes back a fourth time, collecting warnings on Exclusion from the Kingdom, i.e.

$$\begin{aligned} \text{Mt } 5{:}25\text{-}26 &= \text{Lk } 12{:}57\text{-}59 \\ \text{Mt } 7{:}13, 14, 22\text{-}23 &= 13{:}22\text{-}30 \\ &\quad \textit{(cf. also } \text{Mt } 18{:}11\text{-}12\textit{)} \end{aligned}$$

and he goes back a fifth time, for a Parables Section,

$$\begin{aligned} \text{Mt } 5{:}13 &= \text{Lk } 14{:}34\text{-}35 \\ 6{:}24 &= 16{:}13 \end{aligned}$$

and finally for the sixth time, to allocate the remaining fragments,
Mt 5:17-18 = Lk 16:16-17
5:32 = 16:18, which is as it were 'dumped' last of all, and apparently without regard for its context, there being no better place for it!

The other columns of Chart IIB will be found to yield a similar pattern. As regards the material in the intervening chapters,

			Mt		Lk
1) Mt 8 and 9,	we have		8:18-22	=	9:57-62
			9:37-38	=	10:1-12
	back then to		9:32-34	=	11:14 *(but cf. 3) below)*
	back then to		8:11-12	=	13:28-29
2) Mt 10,	we have		10:7-16	=	10:1-15
	back then to		10:40	=	10:16
	back then to		10:26-33	=	12:2-10
	back then to		10:19-20	=	12:11-12
			10:34-36	=	12:49-50
			10:37-38	=	14:25-33
			10:39	=	17:33
3) Mt 11 and 12,	we have		11:20-24	=	10:13-15
			11:25-27	=	10:21-22
			12:22-23	=	11:14 *(but cf. 1) above)*
			12:24-30	=	11:15-23
			12:43-45	=	11:24-26
			12:38-42	=	11:29-32
	then back to		12:31-32	=	12:10
	then back to		11:12-13 (5:17-18)	=	16:16-17
4) Mt 13,	we have		13:16-17	=	10:23-24
			13:31-32	=	13:18-19
			13:33	=	13:20-21
5) Mt 14–17,	we have		16:5-6	=	12:1
	then back to		16:2-3	=	12:54
			17:19-21	=	17:5-6
6) Mt 18,	we have		18:12-24	=	15:1-7
	then back to		18:6-7	=	17:1-3a
			18:15, 21-22	=	17:3b-4
7) Mt 19–22,	we have		22:34-40	=	10:25-28
	then back to		20:16	=	13:30
			22:1-10	=	14:15-24

8) Mt 23 and 24,   Mt   Lk

we have   25:1-13 / 24:43-51 = 12:35-48

then back to   24:17-41 = 17:22-37

Fourthly, more work needs to be done on schematizing the Central Section according to the topics treated in it. The following tentative suggestions are made as a stimulus for further study:

Teaching on Discipleship	9:52–10:37
Teaching on Prayer	10:38–11:13
Teaching on the Good and Bad Spirit	11:14–12:12
Teaching on Worldly Goods	12:13-34
Teaching on Vigilance	12:35–13:17
Teaching on the Kingdom	13:18–16:17
Teaching on Divorce and One's Neighbour	16:18–17:4
Teaching on Faith, Gratitude and Humility	17:5-19
Teaching on the Eschatological Coming of Christ	17:20-37
Teaching on Perseverance in Prayer and Humility	18:1-14

Bibliography on the Central Section

The following books and articles will be found relevant to further discussion:

Blinzler, J., *Die literarische Eigenhart des sogenannten Reiseberichts im Lukasevangelium* in *Syn. Stud.*, München (Karl Zink) 1953, pp. 20-52.

Butler, B. C., *St Luke's Debt to St Matthew* in *Harvard Theological Review* 32 (1939) 237-308.

Cassian, Bishop, *Luke after Matthew but before John* in *Stud. Ev. Texte und Untersch.* 73 (1959).

Conzelmann, H., *The Theology of St Luke*, 1960 (based on 2nd German ed. 1957).

Evans, C. F., *The Central Section of St Luke's Gospel* in *Studies in the Gospels*, ed. D. E. Nineham, Oxford (Blackwell) 1957.

Farrer, A. M., *On Dispensing with "Q"* in *Studies in the Gospels.* ed. D. E. Nineham, Oxford (Blackwell) 1957.

Gasse, W., *Zum Reisebericht des Lukas* in *Z.NT.W.*, (1935) 293-99.

George, A., *Tradition et Rédaction chez Luc: La Construction de la Troisième Evangile* in *De Jésus aux Evangiles*, ed. I. de la Potterie, Louvain, 1967, (*Donum Coppens*).

Girard, L., *L'Evangile des Voyages de Jésus, ou la Section 9:51–18:14 de S. Luc*, Paris 1951.

Grundmann, W., *Fragen der Komposition des lukanischen "Reiseberichts"* in *Z.NT.W.*, (1959) 252-270.

Leal, J., *Los Viajes de Jésus a Jerusalêm segun San Lucas* in *XIV Semana Biblica Espanola*, Madrid 1954, pp. 365-382.
Lohse, E., *Missionarishes Handeln Jesu nach dem Ev. des Lukas* in *Theol. Zeitschrift* 10 (1954) 1-13.
McCown, C. C., *The Geography of Luke's Central Section* in *JBL* 56 (1938) 51-56.
Miyoshi, M., *Der Anfang des Reiseberichts Lk 9:51–10:24* (An. Bi. 60), Rome (Pont. Biblical Institute) 1974.
Morgenthaler, R., *Statistische Synopse*, Zürich/Stuttgart 1971.
Ogg, G., *The Central Section of the Gospel according to St Luke* in *New Testament Studies* 18 (1971) 39-53, which summarises recent views on the nature of the Central Section.
Reicke, B., *Instruction and Discussion in the Travel Narrative* in *Stud. Ev. Texte und Untersch.* 78 (1951) 206-216.
Robinson, W. C. Jr, *The Theological Context for Interpreting Luke and the Travel Narrative* in *JBL*, 1960, Pt 1, pp. 20-31.
Sanday, W., *Studies in the Synoptic Problem*, ed. W. Sanday, Oxford 1911.
Schneider, J., *Zur Analyse des lukanischen Reiseberichts* in *Syn. Stud.*, ed. A. Wikenhauser, München 1953, pp. 207-09.
Wickes, D. R., *The Sources of Luke's Perean Section* in *Hist. and Ling. St. Liter. NT., II Ser.: Ling. and Exeg. Stud.* II/2, 1912.

§4 EXCURSUS ON LUKE'S ADAPTATION OF THE GREAT SERMON – Luke 6:20-49 = Matthew 5–7 : See Chart IIA

We remind ourselves:

1) that Luke's Great Sermon contains as its basis a group of seven units which are part of the seventy or so that are in absolute as well as relative sequence in both Luke and Matthew;

2) that Luke omits altogether eight units of Matthew's Sermon amounting to twenty eight verses. Mark in fact retains two of them, Mk 9:43, 11:25-26. The list of Markan parallels to the Great Sermon are: Mk 4:21 = Lk 11:33 = Mt 5:15; Mk 4:24b = Lk 6:38 = Mt 7:2; Mk 9:43 (45, 47) = Mt 5:27-30; Mk 11:25-26 = Lk 11:1-4 = Mt 6:9-15);

3) that Luke transfers twelve units of Matthew's Great Sermon to suitable places in his Central Section, e.g. the Lord's Prayer to his Prayer Section (10:38–11:13), the 'Light' and 'Sound Eye' units are put together (Lk 11:33-36), and the Anxiety about Earthly Things unit is located in the section devoted to warnings about Attachment to Riches (Lk 12:13-34);

4) hence Luke's Great Sermon contains only some thirty verses as opposed to Matthew's 107; and it is only 28% of the latter's length;
5) Luke's Great Sermon has the same structure as Matthew's, i.e. the same beginning, the same middle and the same ending. Not only are the topics the same but the content too is largely identical. That is to say, Luke has four Beatitudes where Matthew has eight; his middle section teaches the principles of loving one's neighbour (although in a slightly different sequence); and the ending contains similiar ideas and largely identical phraseology, the Tree and its Fruit, Doing the Word, and the House built on a Rock.
6) Luke creates one new unit, his Four Woes, which are clearly not derived from Matthew but must come from another source. In this connection it is worth noting that just as Moses in his final exhortation to the Israelites uttered in the Name of the Lord Four Blessings and Four Curses (Deut. 28:1-6, 15-19), so here Luke makes Jesus, the Giver of the New Law, pronounce Four Blessings and Four Woes (for Jesus never *curses*).

Thus Luke in his own Great Sermon (on the Plain) follows the same sermon pattern as Matthew, making only very minor changes of structure (i.e. the transposition of the Love of Enemies unit and the Golden Rule). He transfers (in order to preserve?) a great deal, in fact twelve units, into suitable contexts in his Central Section (Chart IIB), and makes a number of omissions, most of which are predictable in view of his main object in writing. Finally, he makes one addition (the Four Woes), which actually helps to highlight Matthew's own concept of Jesus as the Giver of the New Law.

There is no space here to compare in detail each individual verse or saying for corroboration of our main thesis, although Luke's treatment of individual words and phrases perfectly accords with his general policy of following Matthew always in spirit and as often as possible in the letter. See for example his adoption of $ἁμαρτωλοί$ for Matthew's $τελῶναι$ at Lk 6:32. Such evidence deserves to be set out in full, but we can only do one thing at a time; and in this book our aim is simply the recognition and clarification of the broad outlines of Luke's dependence on Matthew.

§5 A PROVISIONAL CONCLUSION

Looking back over Part II, which contains the heart of our thesis, we come to the following conclusions:
1) Luke has used five types of sequence arrangement of units in order to achieve his editorial objectives, namely,

a) he has kept sequential parallelism with Matthew in a basic and connected series of units;
b) he has kept a relative sequence in certain other units;
c) he has broken the sequence entirely in three different ways:
   i) by moving certain units into another sequence in his main outline or structure, e.g. the Cleansing of the Leper, 5:12-16;
   ii) he has taken care to avoid sequential parallelism whenever he wished to introduce a unit having the same topic but different content from the Matthean counterpart, e.g. Lk 10:25-28;
   iii) by transferring a large number of units from all over Matthew's Gospel to his Central Section.

2) His editorial purposes in making these sequential alterations can be seen to be, firstly, the creation of a First Preaching Tour of Galilee, secondly, the putting of the Parables' Discourse in a more logical (and probably more chronological) setting, and thirdly, the replacement of Matthew's Teaching Discourses with a complete Teaching Section.

These editorial practices were of course the means by which he aimed to accomplish his main objective, to re-present the Gospel Teaching of Matthew in a form adapted to the needs of the Greek World. They also presuppose, reasonably enough, that the Matthean 'traditions' about Jesus were still susceptible of modification.

We have said above that any sound synoptic theory must explain the dissimilarities as well as the similarities between Matthew and Luke; but the assumption that Luke had Matthew before him to guide him throughout does so by enabling us to see that Luke's editorial activity is intelligent. It is not just simply that Luke shares with Matthew an almost identical framework of similar units, as Table I demonstrates, though this is important enough; it is not just that they have the same topics, but that they have them in basically the same sequence. And what clinches the argument is that Luke not only respects the framework he has borrowed (even when he changes a main element in it, i.e. the Parables' Discourse), but that within this framework he rearranges various units in different patterns (e.g. the First Preaching Tour), and especially by means of a device that he has actually built into it, namely the Central Section. Thus he skilfully keeps vestiges of each of the six Discourses *in situ* and transfers the material he takes out of them mostly to the Central Section, and always purposefully, in order to bring together the Teachings of Jesus in a new collection. The only satisfactory explanation of his procedure is to conclude to his actual possession of our Greek Matthew. There is no need nor room for any intermediate source such as Q. As Butler wrote in connection not with the units but with the vocabulary of Luke, 'there is nothing in Luke which enables us to distinguish the vocabulary of the alleged Q source . . . from that of Matthew.' And again, 'Q, as an explanation of the Matthew-Luke agreements against Mark, is an entirely unneeded and disturbing element in the case; without it . . . a natural solution is provided by the normal application of the principles of comparative literary criticism. And such motiveless patchwork composition (Mt 10:9 = Lk 9:3-5 = Lk 10:4-11 = Mk 6:8-11), as the introduction of Q leads us of necessity to attribute to Matthew, is so improbable psychologically as to constitute a grave objection to the Two-Document solution.'[58] And as Farrer wrote: 'All we have to do to get rid of Q is to make Luke's use of Matthew intelligible.'[59] Although Farrer wrote this in another connection, it remains true that if we have made Luke's use of Matthew intelligible, then Q becomes not only useless but a nuisance.

In other words, we believe that we have succeeded in showing that Luke's transfers of Matthean material — his 'dismemberment' of Matthew — is in fact the work of an intelligent editor working according to a scientific plan for the fulfilment of his main objective. Luke set about refashioning our Greek Matthew according to the following principles: (a) a profound respect for its framework and contents, (b) a willingness to rewrite and amplify the narrative portions in a more cultivated Greek, (c) a separation as far as possible of the narratives from the didactic elements by means of the Central Section, and (d) the removal of doublets and problem passages, and as much as possible of material of solely local Palestinian interest, in order to find room for new stories and anecdotes. The result was our Luke.

Finally, our analysis of Luke's editorial activity in Chapters Six and Seven is strongly supported by our brief examination of his methods in the Centurion's Slave unit, in his First Preaching Tour in Galilee and in his Great Sermon. In each example we see his scrupulous adherence to the Matthean outline, his bold introduction of new units and his rearrangement of existing ones, and his determination to let nothing slip that would be profitable to the Greeks. As regards his Central Section, his adherence to the Matthean outline is seen in his placing it at the one point where it will not disrupt it, namely at the head of the Journey Section; his respect for, and bold handling of, the Matthean material are seen in the way in which he combines and links new units and old. Matthew, following the Pentateuchal tradition which had arranged Moses' teaching in a number of set discourses, arranged the teachings of Jesus in a similar fashion; but Luke, following a modern style, denuded these Discourses to create a major and central Teaching Section.

All these considerations make a strong *prima facie* case for Luke having known and fully utilised our Greek Matthew.

Nevertheless there are many questions about Luke's editorial behaviour yet remaining without an answer, among which are the following:
1) Why does Luke give such diverse treatment to such important items as the Nativity and Resurrection Narratives and the Lord's Prayer?
2) What is the reason for his Great Omission of Mt 14:3—15:29?
3) How do we explain Luke's many detailed additions to many of the Matthean stories about Jesus?
4) What over-all reason can be assigned for Luke's dismemberment and reconstruction of Matthew?

Let us hope that some light on these questions may come from our study of Mark in relation to Luke-with-Matthew; and with these thoughts in mind let us turn to see how the intervention of Mark will qualify our picture and our provisional conclusions.

PART THREE

Mark and Luke-with-Matthew

Part Three : MARK AND LUKE-WITH-MATTHEW

Chapter Nine: How Mark Relates to Luke-with-Matthew: Sequence-agreements and Displacements   72

    Introductory: The Method of this Chapter, and further Explanation of Chart I
1. Fifty-nine Units where all three Gospels have the same sequence
2. One Unit where Mark diverges from the joint sequence of Luke and Matthew (The First Three Days in Jerusalem)
3. Thirteen Units where Mark supports Luke's Change of Matthew's Unit-sequence
4. Seven Units where Mark supports Matthew's Unit-sequence when Luke does not
5. Six Units where Mark alone retains the relative sequence of Matthew
6. Fifteen Units where Mark supports Matthew's Unit-sequence when Luke is lacking
7. Six Units where Mark supports the absolute Unit-sequence of Luke when Matthew is lacking
8. Five Units peculiar to Mark
9. Markan Omissions of Matthean and/or Lukan Units
10. The Meaning of these Unit-sequence Relationships

Chapter Ten: The Imprint of Luke-Matthew on Mark   85
1. The Influence of Luke-Matthew on the Shape of Mark
2. The Minor Divergencies of Mark from Luke-Matthew
3. The Markan Conflations of Lukan and Matthean Expressions
4. Words, Phrases and Sentences added by Mark
5. Conclusion

Chapter Eleven: Some Examples of the Influence of Luke and Matthew on Mark   91
1. Summary of Points to be noted
2. A Simple Test of Mark's Conflationary Tendencies
3. The First Three Days in Jerusalem (The Temple Cleansing)
4. The Raising of Jairus' Daughter
5. The Healing of the Paralytic
6. The Parable of the Sower
7. Herod's Interest in Jesus
8. The Lawyer's Question (The Great Commandment)

Chapter Twelve: The Markan Omissions 110
1. Omissions need not be a Sign of Ignorance
2. The Nativity and Resurrection Narratives, and the Genealogies
3. The Omission of Luke 6:20–8:3 (incl. the Great Sermon)
4. The Omission of the Central Section (9:52–18:14)
5. Markan Omissions of Lukan Glosses on Matthew

CHAPTER NINE

HOW MARK RELATES TO LUKE-WITH-MATTHEW: SEQUENCE-AGREEMENTS AND DISPLACEMENTS

Introductory: the Method of this Chapter: Chart I again

In Part II, on the assumption that Matthew was first and Luke the second Gospel to appear (and Mark not then even thought of), we were able to show that Luke handled the material of Matthew with such a degree of intelligence and skill as to force us to admit that he had our Greek Matthew before his eyes when he composed. If this assumption is correct, there should also be a way in which the third Gospel, Mark, will relate both naturally and reasonably to both Luke and Matthew. Now the Griesbach contention was that Mark in fact had both Luke and Matthew before his eyes when he composed his Gospel.[60] We therefore now proceed to examine the relationship of Mark to Luke-with-Matthew to see if this could really have been the case.

This assumption can be shown diagrammatically thus:

$$\begin{matrix} \text{Mt (Gk)} & \\ \downarrow & \rangle \text{ Mk} \\ \text{Lk} & \end{matrix}$$

We shall now see how it works out in detail.

We again use the method of unit or pericope sequence to lay bare the over-all unit relationship. The assumption behind it is that not only is the original pattern important but also that each individual change made by any evangelist in the sequence is the result of an editorial decision and accordingly has significance for the solution of our problem. We therefore proceed to align Mark against Luke-with-Matthew, i.e. to superimpose the Markan sequence of units upon Chart I, with the result pictured thereon. Here the Markan parallels are indicated by the hatched lines. Thus we have two main sorts of activity, that of Mark, shown by the hatched lines, which indicate his agreement or disagreement with the sequence of Luke and Matthew, and that of Luke, whose agreement or non-agreement with the sequence of Matthew is indicated with the aid of four different kinds of line.[61]

The immediate over-all impression given by Chart I is that Mark is almost invariably in agreement with the sequence of Luke even when Luke changes the sequence of Matthew. Apart from the obvious Markan omissions, the only big exception is Mark's total ignoring of the units found in Luke's Central Section. At the same time Mark is seen to support the common sequence when Luke agrees with Matthew, as he does in by far the larger number of parallel units. Just occasionally Mark, instead of following Luke's divergence from Matthew's sequence, prefers to follow Matthew's sequence. In one instance only does Mark diverge from the joint sequence of Matthew and Luke (i.e. where Matthew and Luke agree against Mark), and that is over the 'Cleansing of the Temple' unit. The meaning of all these sequential relationships will have to be studied, but first we must catalogue the various ways in which Mark relates to the Luke-with-Matthew sequence.

§1 FIFTY-NINE UNITS where Mark supports Luke's unit-sequence, where Luke is already following the sequence of Matthew.

BO §	Title	Mt	Lk	Mk
17	Mission of John	3:1-6	3:1-6	1:2-6
20	The Messiah's Forerunner	3:11-12	3:15-18	1:7-8
22	Baptism of Jesus	3:13-17	3:21-22	1:9-11
24	Temptations of Jesus	4:1-11	4:1-13	1:12-13
36	Jesus returns to Galilee	4:12	4:14-15	1:14
46	First Preaching Tour	4:23	4:44	1:39
57	Great Gathering of Crowds	4:24-25	6:17-19	3:7-12
112	Stilling of the Storm	8:23-27	8:22-25	4:35-41
113	Healing of Gerasene Demoniac	8:28-34	8:26-39	5:1-20
117	Raising of Jairus' Daughter	9:18-26	8:40-56	5:21-43
122	Commissioning of the Twelve	10:1	9:1-2	6:7
124	Commissioning Discourse	10:5-15	9:3-6	6:8-13
159	Herod's Interest in Jesus	14:1-2	9:7-9	6:14-16
162	Feeding of Five Thousand	14:13-21	9:10-17	6:30-44
182	Peter's Confession	16:13-20	9:18-21	8:27-30
183	First Passion Prediction	16:21	9:22	8:31-32a
185	The Cross and Self-Denial	16:24-28	9:23-27	8:34—9:1
186	The Transfiguration	17:1-9	9:28-36	9:2-10
188	Healing of a Possessed Boy	17:14-21	9:37-43a	9:14-29
189	Second Passion Prediction	17:22-23	9:43b-45	9:30-32
191	Discourse on True Greatness	18:1-5	9:46-48	9:33-37
200	Jesus leave Galilee	19:1-2	9:51	10:1
279	'Let little children come'	19:13-15	18:15-17	10:13-16

BO §	Title	Mt	Lk	Mk
280	The Rich Young Man	19:16-22	18:18-23	10:17-22
281	Reward for Leaving All	19:23-30	18:24-30	10:23-31
283	Third Passion Prediction	20:17-19	18:31-34	10:32-34
285	Cure of Beggar/s near Jericho	20:29-34	18:35-43	10:46-52
291	Jesus enters Jerusalem	21:1-9	19:29-40	11:1-10
302	Question of Jesus' Authority	21:23-27	20:1-8	11:27-33
304	Parable of Wicked Tenants	21:33-46	20:9-19	12:1-12
306	Question of Taxes to Caesar	22:15-22	20:20-26	12:13-17
307	Question re Resurrection	22:23-33	20:27-40	12:18-27
309	Question re David's Son	22:41-46	20:41-44	12:35-37
310	Condemnation of Scribes etc.	23:1-14	20:45-47	12:38-40
314	Prediction of Temple's End	24:1-2	21:5-6	13:1-2
315	Signs before the End	24:3-8	21:7-11	13:3-8
316	Persecutions Foretold	24:9-14	21:12-19	13:9-13
317	Prophecy of Calamity	24:15-22	21:20-24	13:14-20
319	Coming of the Son of Man	24:29-31	21:25-28	13:24-27
320	Parable of the Figtree	24:32-33	21:29-31	13:28-29
321	The Time of the Coming	24:34-36	21:32-33	13:30-32
329	Plot to kill Jesus	26:1-5	22:1-2	14:1-2
331	Judas betrays Jesus	26:14-16	22:3-6	14:10-11
332	Preparation for Passover	26:17-19	22:7-13	14:12-16
336	Institution of Eucharist	26:26-28	22:19-20	14:22-24
341	Peter's Denials Foretold	26:33-35	22:33-34	14:29-31
350	Jesus at Gethsemane	26:36-46	22:39-46	14:32-42
351	The Arrest of Jesus	26:47-56	22:47-53	14:43-52
352	Jesus taken to High Priest	26:57-58	22:54-55	14:53-54
360	Morning Council & Condemn.	27:1	23:1	15:1
363	Jesus before Pilate	27:11-14	23:2-5	15:2-5
368	Jesus condemned to Death	27:15-26	23:13-25	15:6-15
369	Mockery of the Soldiers	27:27-32	23:26	15:21
371	The Crucifixion	27:33-44	23:33-43	15:22-32
372	The Death of Jesus	27:45-53	23:44-46	15:33-38
373	The Centurion's Tribute	27:54	23:47	15:39
374	Other Witnesses of J's Death	27:55-56	23:48-49	15:40-41
376	Burial of Jesus	27:57-61	23:50-56	15:42-47
379	Discovery of Empty Tomb	28:1-8	24:1-9	16:1-8

These fifty-nine units are the core of the 'Triple Tradition'. The following features of this group require notice:
1) They are mostly *chreiai* or *apomnemoneumata*, with a few parables.

2) It is precisely with regard to these units that Luke has so much new detail to add to the Matthean version of them.
3) The period covered by these units corresponds to the period of witness of Peter and the rest of the Twelve, i.e. the Public Life of Jesus between the Baptism of John and the Empty Tomb.
4) They contain the basic minimum account of Jesus' life and work.
5) Among these fifty-nine units are some editorial units, which are important for the setting in which Jesus operated. Such are, for example, 'Jesus returns to Galilee' (KA 30), 'The First Preaching Tour' (KA 40), 'The Great Gathering of Crowds' (KA 50), 'Jesus leaves Galilee' (KA 174), 'The Plot to kill Jesus' (KA 305), 'Other Witnesses of Jesus' Death' (KA 348).[62]

§2 ONE UNIT where Mark diverges from the joint sequence of Matthew and Luke,
i.e. where Matthew and Luke agree against Mark or at least are credibly interpreted in this sense according to our Hypothesis.

BO §	Title	Mt	Lk	Mk
293	Jesus Cleanses the Temple	21:12-13	19:45-46	11:15-17

Note 1) that Matthew, Luke and Mark agree absolutely on the sequence of the units: Triumphal Entry, Cleansing of the Temple, Questioning of Jesus' Authority.
2) Luke however omits to describe the reaction of the inhabitants of Jerusalem towards Jesus, and also the cures and excitement that followed the Cleansing; and he also omits the Cursing and Withering of the Figtree (he already has a Figtree parable at 13:6-9).
3) Luke replaces his omissions with two other units, Jesus Weeping over the City, and the Plot of the Priests, neither of which is here paralleled in Matthew.
4) We thus see that Luke deliberately flanks the Cleansing with two other units peculiar to himself. We therefore conclude that Luke deliberately meant his version of the Cleansing to remain parallel to Matthew's. (It is nevertheless true that, owing to Luke's omissions, his Cleansing can still be regarded as parallel to Mark's; yet it seems to us that Luke intended his version to be parallel to Matthew's.)
5) But there can be no ambiguity about the fact that Mark's version of the Cleansing has been deliberately placed in a sequence different from Matthew's, as a result of his splitting the Figtree unit into two sections. See chap. 11 §3 for further discussion.

§3 THIRTEEN UNITS where Mark supports Luke's Changes of Matthew's unit-sequence *(excluding Luke's Central Section)*

BO §	Title	Mt	Lk	Mk
89	Teaching with Authority	7:28-29	4:31-32	1:21-22
109	Healing of Peter's m.-in-law	8:14-15	4:38-39	1:29-31
110	Healings outside the House	8:16-17	4:40-41	1:32-34
90	The Cleansing of a Leper	8:1-4	5:12-16	1:40-45
114	Healing of a Paralytic	9:1-8	5:17-26	2:1-12
115	Calling of Matthew (Levi)	9:9-13	5:27-32	2:13-17
116	A Question about Fasting	9:14-17	5:33-39	2:18-22
135	Plucking Grain on Sabbath	12:1-8	6:1-5	2:23-28
136	Healing of Man with a Withered Hand	12:9-14	6:6-11	3:1-6
145	Preaching in Parables	13:1-3a	8:4	4:1-2
...	Parable of the Sower	13:3b-9	8:5-8	4:3-9
146	Reason for Using Parables	13:10-15	8:9-10	4:10-12
148	Explanation of the Sower	13:18-23	8:11-15	4:13-20

These are also 'Triple Tradition' units because of their parallelism of content. The important thing to notice is that Mark either fully accepts the changes that Luke has made to Matthew's sequence; or else, on the theory of Markan priority, Luke continues to follow Mark, where Matthew deviates in order to follow another unit-sequence.

§4 SEVEN UNITS where Mark supports Matthew's Unit-sequence when Luke does not.

A) *Six Units where Mark supports Matthew's Unit-sequence both absolutely and relatively, where Luke does neither.* [63]

BO §	Title	Mt	Lk	Mk
56/8	Choice of Twelve	5:1	6:12-13	3:13-15
172	Jesus refuses a Sign	16:1-4	12:54-56	8:11-13
173	Leaven of the Pharisees	16:5-12	12:1	8:14-21
193	Warning against Scandal	18:6-9	17:1-2	9:42-48
308	The Lawyer's Question	22:34-40	10:25-28	12:28-34
318	Warning against False Christs	24:23-28	17:22-37	13:21-23

These six units are found, with one exception only, in Luke's Central Section. On Markan Priority, Luke deviates from the Markan sequence which Matthew continues to follow exactly. On my theory and Griesbach's, Mark prefers to follow Matthew's sequence from which Luke has deviated.

B) *One Unit where Mark supports Matthew's sequence both absolutely and relatively, and Luke does neither, but substitutes another story on the same topic in a different sequence.*

BO §	Title	Mt	Lk	Mk
40	Call of Four Fisherman	4:18-22	–	1:16-20
47	Luke's Miraculous Catch	–	5:1-11	–

Here Matthew and Mark are in absolute sequence (see Chart I), but Luke's Miraculous Catch (which is basically a doublet or substitute for the other story) is found in another sequence. Its principal common link (apart from similarity of place, topic, and persons concerned) is Luke's version (5:10) of the saying in Matthew 4:19: 'Come after me and I will make you fishers of men', for which Luke seems to provide the actual *Sitz-im-Leben*. This unit is an example of Luke's practice of transferring to a different sequence from Matthew's a doublet or substitute story that he prefers to the Matthean version of it. For other examples, see the Parable of the Pounds and the Parable of the Mnas, and the Lawyer's Question.

§5 SIX UNITS where Mark aims to retain the relative sequence only of Matthew, and Luke does not.

BO §	Title	Mt	Lk	Mk
56/8, 123	Names of the Twelve	10:2-4	6:14-16	3:16-19
139, 217 98	Jesus and Beelzebul	12:24-30	11:15-23	3:22-27
140	Blasphemy against the Spirit	12:31-32	12:10	3:28-30
144	Anxiety of Mother and Brothers	12:46-50	8:19-21	3:31-35
150	Parable of Mustard Seed	13:31-32	13:18-19	4:30-32
158, 38	Nazareth Visit	13:53-58	4:16-30	6:1-6

These too may be classed as 'Triple Tradition' Units. It will be noted that whereas Luke has adopted a sequence differing from Matthew's with regard to all these units, Mark has in every case placed them in the same relative sequence as in Matthew. This is a very extraordinary thing.

Luke's transposition of the Nazareth Visit to the beginning of his main structure, Lk 4:16-30 (cf. Mt 13:53 = Mk 6:1-6), may also be a further example of his avoiding placing in true parallel his own very different version of this visit; but it can also be seen as an amplification of the reference in Mt 4:13a to Jesus' presence in Nazareth before the opening of the Galilean ministry, and it seems unlikely to be a conflation of the Mt-Mk tradition with his own special tradition about a visit there.

§6 FIFTEEN UNITS where Mark supports Matthew's unit-sequence, when Luke is lacking.

A) *Fourteen Units where Mark has the same absolute sequence as Matthew.*

BO §	Title	Mt	Lk	Mk
160	Execution of John	14:3-12	–	6:19-29
163	Jesus walks on the Water	14:22-33	–	6:45-52
164	Healings at Gennesaret	14:34-36	–	6:53-56
168	The Tradition of the Elders	15:1-20	–	7:1-23
169	Canaanite Woman's Faith	15:21-28	–	7:24-30
171	Feeding of the 4,000	15:32-39	–	8:1-10
184	Peter Rebuked	16:22-23	–	8:32b-33
187	The Coming of Elijah	17:10-13	–	9:11-13
277	On Divorce	19:3-10	–	10:2-9
284	Request of Mother of Sons of Zebedee	20:20-28	–	10:35-45
294	Cursing of Barren Figtree	21:18-19	–	11:12-14
297	Withering of Barren Figtree	21:20-22	–	11:20-24
330	Anointing at Bethany	26:6-13	–	14:3-9
369	Jesus mocked by Soldiers	27:27-31	–	15:16-20

The phenomenon represented by the above units may be legimately understood as Markan support for a number of units which Luke omitted, Mark re-incorporating them in Matthew's sequence.[64]

B) *One Unit where Mark retains the same relative sequence as Matthew, Luke being lacking.*

BO §	Title	Mt	Lk	Mk
152/107	Jesus' Use of Parables	13:34-35	–	4:33-34

It is significant that while Luke's sequence is entirely different as regards the Mustard Seed and the Leaven (adjoining items that are both found in his Central Section at 13:18ff), Mark still follows the relative sequence of Matthew's units. According to Markan priority Matthew is of course said to have kept Mark's sequence. But on my view and Griesbach's, Mark still prefers to follow the relative sequence of Matthew. On the former theory one has to assume that Matthew went to the greatest (and seemingly quite unnecessary) trouble to retain merely the relative

parallels). The parallelism may be set out as follows:

BO §	Titles	Mt	Lk (main)	Lk C/S	Mk
191	On True Greatness	18:1-5	9:46-48	–	9:33-37
192	The Unauthorised Exorcist	–	9:49-50	–	9:38-41
193	Warnings against Scandals	18:6-9	–	17:1-2	9:42-48
61	About Salt	5:13	–	14:34-35	9:49-50

Thus there is no parallel to Mk 9:49-50 in the main narrative of Luke nor in Mt 18, but only in the Great Sermon (Mt 5:13) and in the Central Section at Lk 14:34-35. Moreover Mark gives the 'Salt' metaphor an original turn. Whereas in Mt 'the salt' are the chosen disciples of the Lord, in this passage of Mark the 'salt' becomes just an attribute of the true disciple; they must have salt in themselves and they will be salted through the 'fire' (of persecution?). Mark's use of the term here could be related to the reference to the fire of Gehenna in Mt 18:9; though for Mark 'the fire' is a purifying process; not a destroying one, but a means of 'salting'. The final aphorism, 'Have salt in yourselves, and be at peace with one another' reads more like an addition of Mark's own source than the *ipsissima verba* of Christ.

§9 MARKAN OMISSIONS OF MATTHEAN AND/OR LUKAN UNITS[65]

BO §	Title	Mt	Lk	Mk
4-7	Nativity Narrative and Genealogy	1–2	–	–
9-16	Nativity Narrative	–	1–2	–
18	John condemns Pharisees	3:7-10	3:7-9	–
19	John teaches the Crowds	–	3:10-14	–
23	Genealogy	–	3:23-28	–
59-88	The Great Sermon (on Mount)	5–7	–	–
59-88	Great Sermon (on Plain)	–	6:20-49	–
91	The Centurion's Slave	8:5-13	7:1-10	–
92	The Raising at Naim	–	7:11-17	–
93	John's Envoys	11:2-6	7:18-23	–
94	Jesus praises John	11:7-19	7:24-35	–
95	Anointing by Sinful Woman	–	7:36-50	–
96	The Ministering Women	–	8:1-3	–

BO §	Titles	Mt	Lk	Mk
118	Healing of Two Blind Men	9:27-31	–	–
119	Healing of a Dumb Demoniac	9:32-34	–	–
121	Summary of Jesus' Activity	9:35-38	–	–
134	'Come unto Me'	11:28-30	–	–
137	Jesus the Chosen Servant	12:15-21	–	–
149	Parable of the Weeds	13:24-30	–	–
153	Weeds Parable Explained	13:36-43	–	–
154/6	Parable of Treasure, Pearls, Net	13:44-50	–	–
157	Scribe of New Kingdom	13:51-52	–	–
170	Healing of Many People	15:29-31	–	–
190	The Temple Tax	17:24-27	–	–
196	On Reproving a Brother	18:15-16	–	–
197	Christ in his Church	18:19-20	–	–
199	Par. of Unforgiving Servant	18:23-35	–	–
203-272	The Central Section	–	9:51–18:14	–
278	Teaching on Celibacy	19:10-12	–	–
282	Par. of Workers in Vineyard	20:1-16	–	–
286	Jesus and Zachaeus	–	19:1-10	–
287	Parable of the Pounds	(25:14-29)	19:11-28	–
292	Jesus weeps over the City	–	19:41-44	–
293	Jesus heals in the Temple	21:14-17	–	–
303	Parable of the Two Sons	21:28-32	–	–
305	Parable of the Marriage Feast	22:1-14	(14:15-24)	–
312	Lament over Jerusalem	23:37-39	13:34-35	–
325	Parable of the Talents	25:14-30	(19:11-27)	–
326	Description of L. Judgment	25:31-46	–	–
328	Jesus teaches in the Temple	–	21:37-38	–
362	Suicide of Judas	27:3-10	(Act 1:17-20)	–
364	Jesus before Herod	–	23:6-12	–
378	Jewish Guard at the Tomb	27:62-66	–	–
380/2	Resurrection Appearances	28:9-20	–	–
383/5	Resurrection Appearances	–	24:13-53	–

Comment:
1) Note that Mark omits five units where Luke is found paralleled in Matthew both in topic and content, i.e. KA 14, 85, 106, 107, 285.
2) As regards Luke's Central Section, Mark has no parallels with it,

naum (4:31-32), is not described in Matthew, but the reference to Jesus' departure from Nazareth in Mt 4:13 would have been warrant enough for Luke to insert his new material at that point. Mark on the other hand ignores Luke's early Nazareth Visit and in fact gives a very large degree of support to its place in the later Matthean sequence. For whereas in Mt 13:53-58 (= Mk 6:1-6) we find the later Nazareth Visit placed well after the Missionary Discourse and just before Herod's Sinister Interest in Jesus (Mt 14:1-2), (an interest undoubtedly stimulated by the Mission of the Twelve, Lk 9:1-6), Mark prefers to modify the Matthean sequence to the extent of putting the Visit just before the Sending Forth of the Twelve, a sequence which suits very well the probable development of Jesus' Ministry.

Again, Mark makes the following slight but significant readjustments to the Lukan sequence in the following ways: As regards the Choosing of the Twelve unit and the List of their Names unit, Mark places these two back in the relative sequence of Matthew, i.e. he follows Matthew in putting them after, and not before, the Gathering of the Crowds (Mt 4:24-25). As regards the Jesus and Beelzebul unit and the Sin against the Spirit unit (Mk 3:22-30), which Luke has transferred to his Central Section, Mark follows Matthew's sequence and brings them back into the main framework of the Gospel narrative. It is indeed quite remarkable how often Mark succeeds in retaining as here the Matthean sequence which Luke has felt at liberty to change. Clearly these two units have for Mark, as for Matthew, a special dramatic importance in the general unfolding of Jesus' public life, though Luke has seen fit to relegate them to his Central Section. Similarly, the Parable of the Mustard Seed has been restored by Mark to the main outline, parallel to Matthew's parable section; and Jesus' Use of Parables, omitted by Luke, is retained by Mark in Matthew's sequence; see comment on §6 B) below. Finally, as regards the Anxiety of His Mother and Brethren unit it is hard to see why Luke changed its sequence both absolutely and relatively to Matthew's by placing it after instead of before the Preaching in Parables. Mark has it in the Matthean sequence.

As regards §6 A), we note that Mark retains five Matthean units (Mt 14:22—15:29) that Luke has omitted between Luke 9:17 and 9:18. That is to say, on the assumption that Matthew and Luke were before Mark, Mark made an editorial decision to restore these units which Luke for his own good reasons decided to omit (e.g. possibly to make room for the new material in his Central Section).

As regards the one unit in §6 B), we again note Mark's strong preference for the sequence of Matthew.

As regards §7, we have just seen that whereas in §6 there are fifteen units where Mark supports Matthew in the absence of Luke, here on the contrary we have six units where Mark supports Luke in the absence of Matthew. Three out of the six, as we have seen, are editorial linking passages, and only three are genuine *chreiai* or *apomnemoneumata*. The fact that there are three editorial passages in common in this category goes to show that there is direct literary indebtedness of one Gospel to the other.

Again, Farmer in a short study *The Synoptic Tradition of the Widow's Mite* (*The Synoptic Problem,* pp. 266-270), gives a number of signs of the secondary character of the Marcan form of the tradition as compared to that of Luke, and concludes 'that on strictly form-critical grounds Luke's form is clearly the more original.'

No further comment is required on §8, except to suggest that it indicates that Mark did not aim to add new material.

As to §9, its problems will be considered later in Chapter Twelve. It is enough to say here that harmonisation usually involves the suppression or omission of units that cannot be harmonised or conflated without long explanations that would defeat the purpose of the whole exercise.

We may sum up the findings of this chapter by declaring that they allow us to say that Mark follows the sequence of Matthew far more closely than Luke; in fact, apart from the thirteen instances where Mark accepts Luke's change of Matthew's sequence and the seven units where he only relatively supports the sequence of Matthew, there are no other instances where Mark fails to support fully Matthew's sequence, save the one exception, where (according to our hypothesis) he diverges from both Matthew and Luke over the Cleansing of the Temple sequence, see Chapter Eleven. The facts before us suggest very strongly indeed that the impact of Luke-with-Matthew has determined the actual sequence of units in Mark. There is no doubt then that one valid interpretation of the evidence is that Mark had before his eyes Matthew and Luke in their present unit-sequence.

CHAPTER TEN

THE IMPRINT OF LUKE-MATTHEW ON MARK

We have shown that Mark's sequence can be legitimately interpreted as being determined by his reaction to Luke's treatment of Matthew's sequence. We have seen too how Mark fits in with Luke and Matthew as 'the key into the lock' or as the clasp that draws the two together into a higher unity. The pattern of Luke-with-Matthew has, we say, imposed itself on Mark in various ways. We will examine this influence under the following headings, which correspond to some of the other arguments frequently used to urge the priority of Matthew:

§1 The Influence of Luke-Matthew on the Shape of Mark
§2 The Minor Divergencies of Mark from Luke-Matthew
§3 The Markan Conflations of Lukan and Matthean Expressions
§4 The Addition by Mark of Certain Words, Phrases and Sentences to the Text as found in Luke and Matthew
§5 Conclusion

§1 THE INFLUENCE OF LUKE-MATTHEW ON THE SHAPE OF MARK

A further look at Chart I reveals further connections between the shape of Mark and that of Luke and Matthew. Mark is seen to divide neatly into five blocks:[66]

    I. 1:1–3:19
    II. 3:20–6:13
    III. 6:14–9:50
    IV. 10:1–13:37
    V. 14:1–16:8

Block I takes the story down to the moment at which the Great Sermon is about to begin in the Matthean and Lukan parallels.
Block II begins with the dismay of Jesus' friends and the arrogance of his enemies which leads straight into the Parables' Discourse, and concludes with the Sending Forth of the Twelve to preach the Kingdom.

Block III relates the rest of the Galilean Ministry and ends with the Discourse on Forgiveness and the departure for Judea.
Block IV relates the Ministry in Judea and Jerusalem to the end of the Eschatological Discourse.
Block V relates the Passion, Death and Declaration that Jesus is risen.

We recall how Luke followed exactly the sequence of the six Matthean Discourses, except for switching the Parables' Discourses. We note now how Mark too exactly parallels the Lukan sequence of the Discourses, although he omits the Great Sermon. Moreover Mark follows Luke in summarising Matthean material at the end of a Block, viz. at 3:7-19, 6:8-13, 9:49-50, 13:33-37, as well as at the end of the Parables' Discourse, 4:21-25.

We have also seen that Luke had a special editorial reason for contracting the Matthean Discourses in his main outline, and that he transferred most of the material to his Central Section. Not so with Mark. The Markan 'Mini-Discourses' simply stand in notable isolation, but in the sequence they have in Luke. In other words, Mark has followed Luke's pattern without having his reason for doing so, as he has no Central Section. These Lukan 'Mini-Discourses' are, as we have seen, simply vestiges of the full Matthean Discourses, and the fact that Mark takes them over from Luke without his reason for reducing them must surely mean that he is simply supporting Luke's editorial changes in the Matthean framework. A careful analysis of Lk 8:16-18 = Mk 4:21-25 (see *The Fourfold Gospel Synopsis*) and of Mk 13 will show that Luke has collected materials from different parts of Matthew (for the reasons explained above in Part II) and that Mark has adopted and adapted Luke's version, bringing it incidentally closer to Matthew. This is especially true of the Apocalyptic Discourse in Mark 13.[67] At the same time within this framework, Mark gives total support and harmonisation (where necessary) to the story-units common to Matthew and Luke containing the main materials for the public ministry of Jesus.

§2 THE MINOR DIVERGENCIES OF MARK FROM LUKE AND MATTHEW when all three are in general textual agreement.
(the so-called 'Minor Agreements')

These divergencies are in no sense minor, except as regards actual size; and they have always proved the greatest stumbling-block to the unqualified acceptance of the Priority of Mark, seeing that they provide such a strong argument in favour of (a) Luke knowing Matthew, and (b) of Matthew and Luke not having known Mark, for to do so, they must have arrived at the same time at the identical word or phrase, from which Mark differs, and done so without the advantage of knowing each other. They therefore offer strong corroboration for our hypothesis. As Farmer was to point out devastatingly (*The Synoptic Problem*, chapters 4 and 5), Streeter was never able to cope adequately with them, and only succeeded in a successful 'cover up'.

The most complete list of these 'Minor Agreements' is that of F. Neirynck, *The Minor Agreements of Matthew and Luke against Mark*, Leuven 1975, which however appeared too late for full use. Here is a similar example, which is however typical of the way in which the various types of agreement against Mark, use of the same words, agreement in word order, and so on, are found intertwined.

Thus in the section Mt 21:1-22 = Lk 19:28-48 = Mk 11:1-24 we find the following agreements against Mark:

Mt 21:1	ἤγγισαν ἀπέστειλεν	Lk 19:28	ἤγγισεν ἀπέστειλεν
	Both Mt and Lk omit αὐτοῦ		
:2	λέγων λύσαντες ἀγάγετέ	:30	λέγων λύσαντες ἀγάγετε
:3	ἐρεῖτε ὅτι	:31	ἐρεῖτε· ὅτι
	Both Mt and Lk omit πάλιν ὧδε		
:6	δὲ αὐτοῖς	:32	δὲ αὐτοῖς
	Both omit Mark's δεδεμένον πρὸς θύραν ἔξω ἐπὶ τοῦ ἀμφόδου as well as ἀφῆκαν αὐτούς		
:7	ἤγαγον ἐπ' αὐτῶν ἐπεκάθισεν	:35	ἤγαγον ἐπὶ τὸν πῶλον ἐπεβίβασαν
:8	δὲ ἑαυτῶν ἐν τῇ ὁδῷ	:36	δὲ ἑαυτῶν ἐν τῇ ὁδῷ
:9	δὲ ὄχλοι λέγοντες	:37	δὲ πλῆθος λέγοντες

Both omit Mark's εὐλογημένη ἡ ἐρχομένη βασιλεία τοῦ πατρὸς ἡμῶν Δαυίδ·

Also in verse 37 in Luke and verse 9 in Matthew there is an agreement in meaning (though they use different words) not found in Mark. Mk 11:16 is absent from Mt and Lk and also πᾶσιν τοῖς ἔθνεσιν, 11:17. Also in Mt 21:13b and Lk 19:46b there is an agreement against Mark in word order.

§3 THE MARKAN CONFLATIONS OF MATTHEAN AND LUKAN EXPRESSIONS, or The Duplicate Expressions in Mark.

This category, as Neirynck[68] suggests, can also be regarded either as
a) the avoidance of Markan pleonasms and repetitions by Luke and Matthew, or
b) a two-step conflation in Mark of tradition and redaction, or
c) composite expressions reflecting Mark's own manner of composition.

Neirynck lists these alternative ways of explaining these expressions, which occur with great consistency throughout the Triple Tradition, but none of them offers any explanation of why in so many of these cases Matthew takes the one part and Luke takes the other. By far the easiest explanation, and the one that stares the reader in the face, is that Matthew normally makes a general statement, e.g. that 'it was evening', and that Luke then makes it more precise, i.e. 'the sun had set'; and that Mark for reasons of his own has conflated them both. All we need to do, and will do in due course, is to provide a good reason for Mark's habit of conflation.

Some six random examples are offered below.

	Mt	Lk	Mk
1	8:3b-4a	5:13b-14a	1:41b-44a
	λέγων·	λέγων·	καὶ λέγει αὐτῷ·
	θέλω, καθαρίσθητι.	θέλω, καθαρίσθητι.	θέλω, καθαρίσθητι.
	καὶ εὐθέως ἐκαθαρίσθη	καὶ εὐθέως ἡ λέπρα	⁴²καὶ εὐθὺς ἀπῆλθεν
	αὐτοῦ ἡ λέπρα.	ἀπῆλθεν ἀπ' αὐτοῦ.	ἀπ' αὐτοῦ ἡ λέπρα,
			καὶ ἐκαθαρίσθη.
			⁴³καὶ ἐμβριμησάμενος
			αὐτῷ εὐθὺς ἐξέβαλεν
	⁴καὶ λέγει	¹⁴καὶ αὐτὸς	αὐτόν. ⁴⁴καὶ λέγει
	αὐτῷ ὁ Ἰησοῦς·	παρήγγειλεν αὐτῷ·	αὐτῷ·
2	4:1-2	4:1-2	1:12-13
	τότε ὁ Ἰησοῦς ἀνήχθη	Ἰησοῦς δὲ πλήρης	καὶ εὐθὺς τὸ
	εἰς τὴν ἔρημον ὑπὸ	πνεύματος ἁγίου	πνεῦμα αὐτὸν ἐκβάλλει
	τοῦ πνεύματος πειρασ-	ὑπέστρεψεν ἀπὸ τοῦ	εἰς τὴν ἔρημον.
	θῆναι ὑπὸ τοῦ διαβόλου,	Ἰορδάνου, καὶ ἤγετο	¹³καὶ ἦν ἐν τῇ ἐρήμῳ
		ἐν τῷ πνεύματι ἐν τῇ	τεσσεράκοντα ἡμέρας
		ἐρήμῳ.	πειραζόμενος
	²καὶ νηστεύσας ἡμέρας	²ἡμέρας	
	τεσσεράκοντα καὶ	τεσσεράκοντα πειρα-	
	τεσσεράκοντα νύκτας	ζόμενος ὑπὸ τοῦ	ὑπὸ τοῦ
	ὕστερον ἐπείνασεν.	διαβόλου. καὶ οὐκ	σατανᾶ, καὶ ἦν μετὰ
		ἔφαγεν οὐδὲν...	τῶν θηρίων,

	Mt	Lk	Mk
3	8:16	4:40	1:32
	Ὀψίας δὲ γενομένης	Δύνοντος δὲ τοῦ ἡλίου	Ὀψίας δὲ γενομένης ὅτε ἔδυσεν ὁ ἥλιος
4	20:29	18:35	10:46
	Καὶ ἐκπορευομένων αὐτῶν ἀπὸ Ἰεριχὼ	Ἐγένετο δὲ ἐν τῷ ἐγγίζειν αὐτὸν εἰς Ἰεριχὼ	Καὶ ἔρχονται εἰς Ἰεριχώ. καὶ ἐκπορευομένου αὐτοῦ ἀπὸ Ἰεριχὼ
5	26:2	22:1	14:1
	οἴδατε ὅτι μετὰ δύο ἡμέρας τὸ πάσχα γίνεται,	Ἤγγιζεν δὲ ἡ ἑορτὴ τῶν ἀζύμων ἡ λεγομένη πάσχα.	Ἦν δὲ τὸ πάσχα καὶ τὰ ἄζυμα μετὰ δύο ἡμέρας.
6	26:17	22:7	14:12
	τῇ δὲ πρώτῃ τῶν ἀζύμων	Ἦλθεο δὲ ἡμέρα τῶν ἀζύμων, ἐν ᾗ ἔδει θύεσθαι τὸ πάσχα,	Καὶ τῇ πρώτῃ ἡμέρᾳ τῶν ἀζύμων, ὅτε τὸ πάσχα ἔθυον.

I comment on two only:

1. In this example (Mt 8:3 and parallels) there are two particularly clear examples of Markan conflation and of progressive development of a statement from Matthew, through Luke to Mark. They occur in successive verses.

a) The example of conflation is Mt 8:3b = Lk 5:13c = Mk 1:42:
   Mt has: 'And straightaway his leprosy was cleansed.'
   Lk has: 'And straightaway his leprosy departed from him.'
   Mk has: 'Straightaway his leprosy departed from him and he was cleansed.'

b) The example of progressive development (and conflation too) of a statement is at Mt 8:4a = Lk 5:14a = Mk 1:43-44a, as follows:
   Mt has: 'And Jesus says to him:'
   Lk has: 'And he commanded him:'
   Mk has: 'And getting very excited with him he cast him out, and says to him:'

Assuming as we must the close literary connection between the three Gospels, and putting these two examples together, it is almost impossible to visualise any other sequence, but that of Luke developing Matthew and of Mark expanding both.

4. The fourth example, Mk 10:46 and parallels, is particularly interesting as it shows Mark conflating and trying to reconcile the apparently divergent statements of Matthew and Luke.

§4 THE ADDITION BY MARK OF CERTAIN WORDS, PHRASES AND SENTENCES to the Text as found in Matthew and Luke
(or the Joint Omission by Luke and Matthew of certain Words, Phrases and Sentences of Mark.)

Such are: Mk 2:27 ('The Sabbath was made for man, not man for the Sabbath'), and Mk 5:13 ὡς δισχίλιοι ('about two thousand' swine). If Mark was not adding to the joint narratives of Matthew and Luke, we have to assume that each independently agreed to omit these fascinating details, without of course either knowing what the other was going to do. Further examples are to be found in almost every single unit of the Triple Tradition.

§5 CONCLUSION

Our brief summary of the evidence for Mark's use of both Luke and Matthew continues to strengthen our view that Mark can be truly envisaged as harmonising Luke with Matthew in various ways and especially by conflation. Such conflation involves, as we shall learn in the next chapter from practical examples, not just accepting the actual sequence of first one and then the other, but a parallel process within each unit by which Mark discriminates between what he will accept of Luke's additions to Matthew, what he decides to add or to explain for his own part, and what he judges to be Lukan glosses and therefore decides to omit. In fact his principles of harmonisation are to be seen at work as much in his decisions about omission as about inclusion. See Chapter Twelve for a fuller discussion of the Markan Omissions.

CHAPTER ELEVEN

SOME EXAMPLES OF THE IMPRINT OF LUKE AND MATTHEW ON MARK

§ 1 SUMMARY OF SOME CHARACTERISTICS TO BE NOTED

We are now in a position to examine with profit some representative units of the 'Triple Tradition'. The following observations would appear to hold true for all its major units, including the ones to be now exemplified:

1) In Matthew the story is always told in the fewest possible words, in Luke's version it is always longer, and in Mark's is longest of all. There is in fact a progressive development and expansion of each story from Matthew through Luke to Mark.

2) Luke often adds a few words of introduction to a unit, which Mark usually takes for granted and does not as a rule repeat, but tends to add other consonant detail. Luke always gives a preliminary indication when he has transferred a Matthean unit or block of units.

3) Luke's version contains everything that Matthew's has and adds further detail. Mark too has everything that Matthew has and also has almost everything that Luke adds.

4) Mark often adds extra details of his own, some vivid, others only secondary, thus bringing the whole scene into still clearer focus. There is thus a progressive clarification of detail from Matthew through Luke to Mark.

5) Mark is continually conflating Luke's words and phrases with Matthew's.

6) Noteworthy too is Mark's independent viewpoint; for he makes not infrequent *précisions* both to Luke and to Matthew, and always omits Luke's editorial comments and glosses.

All these six characteristics will be considered with respect to each of the following units.

§2 A SIMPLE TEST OF MARK'S CONFLATIONARY TENDENCIES

If, as we suspect, one of Mark's main objects was to harmonise

Luke's units with Matthew's, we should expect Mark to behave differently when he is conflating or harmonising Luke with Matthew from when he is paralleling either Luke or Matthew alone. When we look closely we shall find that:

1) When Mark has a unit parallel to Luke, Matthew being absent, Mark adds very little to Luke beyond giving evidence of secondary verbal additions, together with the occasional vivid detail.

2) When Mark has a unit parallel to one of Matthew's, Luke being absent, Mark again adds very little to Matthew except for some rephrasing of the narrative, and the occasional vivid eye-witness detail (there are four exceptions to this generalisation that will be dealt with).

That is to say that when Mark is in 'double tradition' with either Matthew alone or with Luke alone, he basically follows Matthew and Luke respectively.

3) But when Mark parallels Luke and Matthew in the 'Triple Tradition', he always has all the extra material that Luke has added to Matthew, or its equivalent.

The conclusion to be drawn from these phenomena is that Mark is conflating Luke with Matthew whenever all three relate the same unit, and the amount of Mark's addition to Matthew, will depend on how much Luke has himself added to Matthew's story.

That this conclusion is true can easily be verified from the data we have already given, and from the examples to follow.

As to 1), Chapter Nine, §7 contains a list of six units where Mark and Luke are alone in the Double Tradition. Of these, three are editorial units and three are story units. All six exhibit the characteristics we have mentioned above, though we have no room to elaborate here.

As to 2), there are in all some fourteen units involved, see Chapter Nine, §6A. In ten of them, it is quite clear that Mark closely follows Matthew and has only minor secondary additions and the occasional eye-witness detail. There are however four units that seem to be exceptions, and a brief word must be said about each. They are:

The Execution of John the Baptist (Mt 14:3-12 = Mk 6:19-29)
In this unit it is clear that although Mark follows the pattern of Matthew's story he has some new detail to add from his own sources.

The Tradition of the Elders (Mt 15:1-20 = Mk 7:1-23)
Here, it is true that Mark has some considerable additions to Matthew, but they are also all secondary in the sense that they are *explanatory*, giving the background necessary for a Greco-Roman audience to comprehend Jesus' teaching, e.g. 7:2-4, 19c. Mark also omits the difficult saying of Matthew's vv. 12b-15a.

The Healing of the Syro-Phoenician's Daughter (Mt 15:21-28 = Mark 7:24-30)
Here although the story is very similar in both accounts, Mark leaves out Matthew's vv. 23 and 24, which appear to be derogatory to Gentiles.

The Teaching on Divorce (Mt 19:3-10 = Mk 10:2-9)
Here the problem is different. For Mark and Matthew agree very closely, except for the fact that Mark omits Matthew's exceptive clause μὴ ἐπὶ πορνείᾳ, thus making the prohibition of divorce absolute.

This Markan omission is usually taken to be strong evidence in favour of the priority of Mark. For it is argued that *a priori* it is much more likely that there was a regression to Matthew's 'laxer' view than vice versa. The argument is however by no means convincing and can be easily turned round. For firstly Paul, who is earlier than Mark, agrees with Mark (I Cor. 7:10-11), and so does Luke (16:18), who is Matthew's contemporary. There was therefore an absolutely primitive tradition that the Lord had altogether prohibited divorce. It must also be understood that Jesus was answering a technical rabbinic question in the same technical language. It is therefore arguable that Matthew understood perfectly well what the Lord had intended and that the exceptive clause was not meant to be taken as permitting divorce for unfaithfulness. Mark's removal of the exceptive clause can be understood as a deliberate act of interpretation because the clause was being wrongly invoked or misunderstood. The source behind Mark is certainly authoritative (one has only to think of Mk 7:19c καθαρίζων πάντα τὰ βρώματα, his correction of Mt at Mk 11:10f., and possibly 2:27 'The Sabbath was made for man and not man for the Sabbath'). The argument for holding that Mark deliberately omitted the Exception Clause is that pastoral experience had confirmed Mark's Church (and Luke's) in the view that it was a stumbling block to the clear teaching of Jesus against divorce. That Mark should behave in this way does not in fact surprise us at all in view of our thesis that he constantly sits in judgment on Luke's treatment of Matthew, cf. his treatment of Mt 21:10-22 and parallels.

We may therefore conclude that these seeming exceptions do no more than show that Mark had also in mind other aspects of the Matthew-Luke relationship as well as that of harmonising. For it would seem that when confronted with Matthew and Luke together, Mark behaves very differently from when he is dealing with either separately.

§3 THE FIRST THREE DAYS IN JERUSALEM
(Mt 21:10-22 = Lk 19:45-48 = Mk 11:11-24) (BO 293/4, 297)

A careful comparison of the Synopses of Huck (6 .edn), Sparks

(1964/70), and Aland (7 edn, 1971), shows that there is no unanimity of treatment in regard to this passage of the Synoptics.[69] The problem arises partly from the fact that while Luke omits altogether the Cursing and Withering of the Figtree in this context, Mark divides it into two parts occurring on succeeding days, while Matthew makes it into one unit only occurring on the first day; and partly from the fact that the only item in this whole section that belongs to the Triple Tradition is the Cleansing of the Temple unit, which Mark records in a sequence different from that of Luke and Matthew. On the supposition that Luke followed Matthew this unit is to be viewed as the sole Major Agreement of sequence of Matthew and Luke against Mark, in contradistinction to the literally hundreds of Minor Agreements that they have in common against Mark. In other words, this may be a case where Mark diverges from Matthew and Luke when they agree together.[70]

The following comments must be made on the three parallel accounts:
1) Note that all three Gospels concur in the same absolute and relative sequence for the Triumphal Approach to Jerusalem unit (Mt 21:1-9 = Lk 19:28-40 = Mk 11:1-10) and again at Mt 21:23-27 = Lk 20:1-8 = Mk 11:27-33. Luke also adds his 19:41-44, the anecdote of Jesus weeping over the City, which is not paralleled in Matthew or Mark. (The parallel to Mt 23:37-39 is Lk 13:34-35.)
2) Matthew then describes the wonder and excitement caused by Jesus' arrival in the Holy City, and the inquiries of the crowd about him, vv. 10-11. Luke has no parallel to this, but Mark speaks of Jesus going not only into Jerusalem but also paying a preliminary visit of inspection to the Temple, 'And he entered into Jerusalem, into the Temple, and looking around at all things ($\pi\epsilon\rho\iota\beta\lambda\epsilon\psi\acute{\alpha}\mu\epsilon\nu o\varsigma$ $\pi\acute{\alpha}\nu\tau\alpha$), the evening hour being already at hand, he went out to Bethany with his disciples.' (v. 11)
3) Thus Mark makes it quite clear that Jesus did nothing more of note on the day of his arrival (Day One) than carefully inspect the Temple precincts.
4) Matthew however in his usual way, it seems, 'telescoped' or closed up the succession of events by relating the Cleansing of the Temple as if it had happened on that very day, vv. 12-13, and goes on to describe the joy of the people and the children at what he had done and at the healings he performed, vv. 14-16. Mark and Luke omit this description.
5) Luke's sequence agrees with Matthew's, though his own tradition has no material to add here.
6) Then in his next verse, v. 17, Matthew relates that Jesus 'left them and went out of the city to Bethany and stayed there', and this is clearly parallel to Mk 11:11b.

The First Three Days in Jerusalem : Unit Chart			
Unit	Mt 21	Lk 19	Mk 11
Entry	1-9 ————	29-40 ————	1-10
Jesus weeps	–	41-44	–
In the City	10-11	....	11a
Cleansing of Temple	12-13 ————	45-46	–
Jesus' Healings	14-16	–	–
To Bethany	17	....	11b
Cursing of Figtree	18-19	....	12-14
	–	– Cleansing of Temple	15-17
Plot	–	47-48 ————	18
He goes out again	–	–	19
Fig-tree Withered	20-22	....	20-24
On Forgiveness	(6:14-15)	–	25-26
Jesus' Authority	23-27 ————	20:1-8 ————	27-33

7) Consequently we find Matthew and Mark in exact step the next morning when Jesus returns to the City, Mt 21:18-19 = Mk 11:12-14. Both agree that the figtree was cursed on the way into the City in the morning, but for Mark this happened before the Cleansing. And here again we have another example of Matthew shortening the perspective by relating consecutively the Cursing and the Discovery of the Withering of the Figtree, which Mark places on consecutive mornings. In between, on his Second Day in Jerusalem, Mark places the Expulsion of the Buyers and Sellers, v. 15.

8) Mark's account of the Expulsion is certainly the same incident as the one already described above in Matthew and Luke.

9) At this point only Luke and Mark add the detail that the High Priests and the Scribes became incensed and planned to do away with Jesus, Lk 19:47-48 = Mk 11:18.

10) Mark alone then expressly mentions that again 'when evening came Jesus withdrew from the City', v. 19.

11) It is only Mark who links the two parts of the story by relating that 'passing by in the morning they saw the figtree withered', v. 20, and the

Markan narrative then joins up with Matthew's at the point where Mark had previously left off; and finally, both accounts go on to relate the moral that Jesus drew from this strange event, namely, the value and cogency of the prayer of faith. Mark last of all adds a rider, v. 24, that is only paralleled at Mt 6:14-15.

12) The difference in the timetabling of the occurrences may be shown thus:

First Day—Matthew and Luke	First Day—Mark
Triumphal Entry into Jerusalem and into the Temple.	Triumphal Entry into Jerusalem and into the Temple. Jesus inspects everything; then retires to Bethany for the night.
	Second Day
	While returning to the City in the morning, Jesus sees and curses the Barren Figtree.
While in the Temple, Jesus expels the buyers and sellers. There is general rejoicing by the people. (Mt only)	He re-enters the Temple and expels the buyers and sellers.
The High Priests are bitterly incensed, and plot against him. Jesus retires to Bethany, where he resides. (Lk only)	The High priests are bitterly incensed, and plot against him. Jesus again retires to Bethany.
Second Day	
In the morning on his way into the City, Jesus sees and curses the Barren Figtree. (Mt only)	
	Third Day
When the disciples saw the figtree withered, they wondered, and asked Jesus for an explanation, etc. They again enter the Temple (Mt 21:23ff, and Lk 20:1f) and are challenged by the High Priests.	In the morning passing by, the disciples saw the figtree withered, and wondered and asked Jesus for an explanation, etc. They again enter the Temple, and are challenged by the High Priests. (v.27)

This analysis seems to suggest that Mark has composed his narrative so as to give good reason why he has split Matthew's narrative of the Figtree into two parts; it is because Mark knows that the Cleansing of the Temple came exactly between them.

Mark's narrative carefully distinguishes three days, three consecutive visits relating what happened on each day, and expressly mentions two returns to Bethany. He could not be more precise about Jesus' movements during this period. Luke on the other hand has little to offer to this anecdote, only the plotting of the High Priests after the Expulsion, and barely supports the Matthean narrative, which in its turn leaves one a little bewildered by his foreshortening of the perspective. Mark however by his clarifications of Jesus' movements helps us a great deal to understand the rationality of Jesus' actions by unfolding the exact order and progression of events. Mark in effect explains that on the original day of entry, there was no time (on account of the late hour) for Jesus to do more than make a careful tour of inspection to see for himself how the place was being run and note the abuses that the Messiah would have to deal with, see Mal 3:1-3. Having seen for himself what needed to be done, he retired to Bethany for the night.

Furthermore, the Markan arrangement of the Barren Figtree unit is far more credible than Matthew's. It is true that from the form critical angle the Matthean form is more likely to be earlier than the Markan, and with this we agree. But from the angle of literary criticism, it is also easier to hold that the compiler of the original Matthean unit was in fact fusing together a story that in reality had consisted of the two parts that we find in Mark. For it seems most unlikely that the tree was actually seen to wither before the very eyes of the disciples, nor does the narrative of Matthew compel us to think so. But given Jesus' miraculous power to effect by a word the withering of the life of the tree, the effect of his word would surely take in the course of nature some hours to become visible. In other words there can be little doubt that the event took place in two parts as Mark relates. It was also an acted parable by which he revealed his foreboding that the High Priesthood would adopt a course that would wither the future of 'the Israel according to the flesh'. It was indeed meant to be a sign, that would be later recalled, of the tragedy that was to come to pass.

In the light of this web of relationships between Mark and Matthew-with-Luke, can we see in which direction the indebtedness lies? Is it, for example, at all realistic to hold that Matthew or Luke have used or even known Mark's version of this section? There is no likelihood at all of either being derived from Mark. On the contrary, the most sensible way of looking at their relationship is to see Mark's version as elicited by the problems caused by the foreshortening and telescoping of the events as narrated in Matthew, whom Luke follows. This text seems therefore conclusive for Mark having known and reacted to the Matthean version in the way we have seen.

§4 THE RAISING OF JAIRUS' DAUGHTER
(Mt 9:18-26 = Lk 8:40-55 = Mk 5:21-43 : BO 117)

A careful examination of these verses in parallel gives rise to the following observations:

1) It is quite clear that Matthew's text is the shortest, that Luke is next in length, and that Mark is the longest. Note too that Matthew does not need to define who a 'ruler' is, since it assumes a Jewish theological background.

2) Luke's introductory words are helpful in setting the scene; Mark completes by adding that 'he was by the sea'.

3) Luke omits nothing that Matthew has save his v. 21 (which Mark supplies), but his additions reveal that Matthew has greatly compressed what must have actually happened. Hence Luke's re-telling is more than justified by the way in which he opens up and fills in the missing developments. Matthew, for example, relates that the ruler says that his daughter has just died, whereas in the parallel passage in Luke she is 'about to die' (and so in Mark). For Matthew in his abbreviated account has omitted the arrival of the messenger to announce the child's death, yet confines his words to the latter occasion, so that his 'has just died' is in fact absolutely accurate. Matthew's account is indeed a precis of the facts, but it is not necessary to assume that he made it from Mark, or even that he made it himself; he is just as likely to have inherited it from his own source. For it is much harder to understand Matthew as abbreviating Mark than Luke as expanding Matthew, with Mark subsequently taking just about everything that Luke has added.

4) Mark however adds even more to the extra details added by Luke. Take Matthew's v. 20a for example and its parallels for Mark's extra vivid personal detail. Other vivid Markan details are: 'Looking round to see who had done it', v. 32; 'Jesus overheard the announcement (that the child had just died)', v. 36. In general however Mark corroborates all the new information brought in by Luke, save a few secondary details, e.g $\mu o \nu o \gamma \epsilon \nu \grave{\eta} \varsigma$ (v. 42), $\tau o \hat{u} \ \kappa \rho a \sigma \pi \acute{\epsilon} \delta o u$ (v. 44), $\pi o \lambda \lambda \grave{a}$ (v. 23). Mark also corroborates Matthew's v. 21 which Luke omits.

5) Mark is regularly conflating Luke's words and phrases with Matthew's. In Mt 9:19 = Lk 8:42b = Mk 5:24, we have a good example of Mark's

conflating tendency. In Matthew Jesus 'follows the ruler and his disciples follow him'; but in Luke we have, 'And as he went off the crowds suffocated him'. However in Mark we have, 'And Jesus *went* away with him, and a large crowd *followed* him and thronged him'. Another example is in Mk 5:42 and parallels.

6) Mark's independent viewpoint is illustrated in the following ways:

a) Whereas Luke adds Peter's own personal reaction to Jesus' question, 'Who touched me?', Mark omits this but instead adds his own v. 31, the reaction of the disciples as a group. Note too how Mark summarises Luke's v. 47b in the three words πᾶσαν τὴν ἀληθείαν.

b) Mark makes the sequence of events more precise by explaining that Jesus took into the house with him only three of the disciples, Peter, James and John, and he also explicitates that the same three with the parents were alone admitted to the bedroom of the dead girl (v. 40).

c) Mark omits two Lukan glosses on the story, viz. '(the woman) seeing she was not hidden', v. 47a, and 'and her spirit returned', v. 55a. We also note Mark paraphrasing Matthew's v. 22b by putting it into direct speech.

d) See Luke's v. 44b (lacking in Matthew) where Mark adds his own most interesting comment, v. 29a-30, revealing that the woman's own personal knowledge of her cure is paralleled by Jesus' own awareness that power to cure has gone forth from him.

§5 THE HEALING OF THE PARALYTIC
(Mt 9:1-8 = Lk 5:17-26 = Mk 2:1-12 : BO 114)

1) Again, Matthew's version is the shortest, Luke's is next in length, and Mark's is the longest.

2) Luke's 'And it came to pass on one of the days', is, as we have seen, an indication of its displacement by Luke, who also adds some helpful words of introduction to the whole story, v. 17, which Mark assumes when he adds that the house was crammed 'to the door', v. 1.

3) Luke has everything that Matthew has, and Mark also. Luke has much extra that Matthew has not, which Mark also has.

4) Mark's extra details consist chiefly in two points. In v. 4 he speaks of 'digging through' the turf roof, where Luke, accommodating himself to his Gentile audience, speaks of 'removing the tiles', And Mark insists (Luke is not quite clear) that Jesus knew 'in his spirit' the charges being framed against him by the Pharisees and Scribes seated in front of him, v. 8., cf. Chapter 4, §1. Again Mark alone mentions that there were four stretcher-bearers.

5) Mark's conflationary tendency can be seen in his v. 6.
6) Mark's independent view-point can be seen most clearly in his insistence that Jesus knew 'in his spirit' what was being said against him. Cf. in the previous example, that 'power had gone forth from him', Mk 5:30.

§6 THE PARABLE OF THE SOWER
(Mt 13:1-9 = Lk 8:4-8 = Mk 4:1-9 : BO 145)

Mt 13:1-9	Lk 8:4-8	Mk 4:1-9
¹ Ἐν τῇ ἡμέρᾳ ἐκείνῃ ἐξελθὼν ὁ Ἰησοῦς τῆς οἰκίας ἐκάθητο παρὰ τὴν θάλασσαν· ² καὶ συνήχθησαν πρὸς αὐτὸν ὄχλοι πολλοί,	⁴ Συνιόντος δὲ ὄχλου πολλοῦ καὶ τῶν κατὰ πόλιν ἐπιπορευομένων πρὸς αὐτὸν	¹ καὶ πάλιν ἤρξατο διδάσκειν παρὰ τὴν θάλασσαν· καὶ συνάγεται πρὸς αὐτὸν ὄχλος πλεῖστος,
ὥστε αὐτὸν εἰς πλοῖον ἐμβάντα καθῆσθαι, καὶ πᾶς ὁ ὄχλος ἐπὶ τὸν αἰγιαλὸν εἰστήκει. ³ καὶ ἐλάλησεν αὐτοῖς πολλὰ ἐν παραβολαῖς λέγων·	εἶπεν διὰ παραβολῆς·	ὥστε αὐτὸν εἰς πλοῖον ἐμβάντα καθῆσθαι ἐν τῇ θαλάσσῃ καὶ πᾶς ὁ ὄχλος πρὸς τὴν θάλασσαν ἐπὶ τῆς γῆς ἦσαν. ² καὶ ἐδίδασκεν αὐτοὺς ἐν παραβολαῖς πολλά, καὶ ἔλεγεν αὐτοῖς ἐν τῇ διδαχῇ αὐτοῦ· ³ἀκούετε.
Ἰδοὺ ἐξῆλθεν ὁ σπείρων τοῦ σπείρειν.	⁵ ἐξῆλθεν ὁ σπείρων τοῦ σπεῖραι τὸν σπόρον αὐτοῦ.	ἰδοὺ ἐξῆλθεν ὁ σπείρων σπεῖραι.
⁴ καὶ ἐν τῷ σπείρειν αὐτὸν ἃ μὲν ἔπεσεν παρὰ τὴν ὁδόν, καὶ ἐλθόντα τὰ πετεινὰ κατέφαγεν αὐτά. ⁵ ἄλλα δὲ ἔπεσεν ἐπὶ τὰ πετρώδη	καὶ ἐν τῷ σπείρειν αὐτὸν ὃ μὲν ἔπεσεν παρὰ τὴν ὁδόν, καὶ κατεπατήθη, καὶ τὰ πετεινὰ τοῦ οὐρανοῦ κατέφαγεν αὐτό. ⁶ καὶ ἕτερον κατέπεσεν ἐπὶ τὴν πέτραν,	⁴ καὶ ἐγένετο ἐν τῷ σπείρειν ὃ μὲν ἔπεσεν παρὰ τὴν ὁδόν, καὶ ἦλθεν τὰ πετεινὰ καὶ κατέφαγεν αὐτό. ⁵ καὶ ἄλλο ἔπεσεν ἐπὶ τὸ πετρῶδες

Mt 13:1-9	Lk 8:4-8	Mk 4:1-9
ὅπου οὐκ εἶχεν γῆν πολλήν, καὶ εὐθέως ἐξανέτειλεν διὰ τὸ μὴ ἔχειν βάθος γῆς· ⁶ἡλίου δὲ ἀνατείλαντος ἐκαυματίσθη, καὶ διὰ τὸ μὴ ἔχειν ῥίζαν ἐξηράνθη. ⁷ἄλλα δὲ ἔπεσεν ἐπὶ τὰς ἀκάνθας, καὶ ἀνέβησαν αἱ ἄκανθαι καὶ ἀπέπνιξαν αὐτά. ⁸ἄλλα δὲ ἔπεσεν ἐπὶ τὴν γῆν τὴν καλὴν καὶ ἐδίδου καρπόν, ὃ μὲν ἑκατόν, ὃ δὲ ἑξήκοντα, ὃ δὲ τριάκοντα. ⁹ὁ ἔχων ὦτα [ἀκούειν] ἀκουέτω.	καὶ φυὲν ἐξηράνθη διὰ τὸ μὴ ἔχειν ἰκμάδα. ⁷καὶ ἕτερον ἔπεσεν ἐν μέσῳ τῶν ἀκανθῶν, καὶ συμφυεῖσαι αἱ ἄκανθαι ἀπέπνιξαν αὐτό. ⁸καὶ ἕτερον ἔπεσεν εἰς τὴν γῆν τὴν ἀγαθὴν καὶ φυὲν ἐποίησεν καρπὸν ἑκατονταπλασίονα. ταῦτα λέγων ἐφώνει· ὁ ἔχων ὦτα ἀκούειν ἀκουέτω.	ὅπου οὐκ εἶχεν γῆν πολλήν, καὶ εὐθὺς ἐξανέτειλεν διὰ τὸ μὴ ἔχειν βάθος γῆς· ⁶καὶ ὅτε ἀνέτειλεν ὁ ἥλιος ἐκαυματίσθη, καὶ διὰ τὸ μὴ ἔχειν ῥίζαν ἐξηράνθη. ⁷καὶ ἄλλο ἔπεσεν εἰς τὰς ἀκάνθας, καὶ ἀνέβησαν αἱ ἄκανθαι καὶ συνέπνιξαν αὐτό, καὶ καρπὸν οὐκ ἔδωκεν. ⁸καὶ ἄλλα ἔπεσεν εἰς τὴν γῆν τὴν καλὴν καὶ ἐδίδου καρπὸν ἀναβαίνοντα καὶ αὐξανόμενα καὶ ἔφερεν εἰς τριάκοντα, καὶ ἐν ἑξήκοντα, καὶ ἐν ἑκατόν. ⁹καὶ ἔλεγεν· ὃς ἔχει ὦτα ἀκούειν ἀκουέτω.

1) This is one of the very few cases where Luke is shorter than Matthew or Mark; Matthew in fact has 91 words in the parable itself; Luke only 75 and Mark 101. The reason is not far to seek; Luke has effected a drastic economy of words in v. 6, where he uses two words καὶ φυὲν, for Matthew's 17 and Mark's 19. Also in v. 8, Luke uses the more literary ἑκατονταπλασίονα for the Matthean phrase, incidentally saving eight words on Matthew and seven on Mark.

2) Again in the introduction to this unit, Luke is shorter and less elaborate than the other two. We must recall that according to our hypothesis, he is abbreviating the Parables' Discourse, as he does the

other Discourses of Matthew, and transfers two parables to the Central Section. Note too that whereas Matthew writes 'parables' because he gives us seven, and Mark 'parables' because he gives us three, Luke writes 'by a parable' because in this context he gives us only this one. Finally the vagueness of Luke's introduction, v. 4, shows that there is no continuity of events between this and the preceding unit.

3) Nevertheless, despite his economical use of words, Luke has retained the full sense of the parable, if not the vivid colour of Matthew and Mark. Luke also has three small additions, which are meant to be explanatory; κατεπατήθη, which explains why the seed did not take root, πετεινὰ τοῦ οὐρανοῦ, which explains that 'winged creatures of the sky', means the birds, and not 'winged things of the earth' i.e. insects.

Indeed, a careful study of v. 6 reveals that despite its brevity it contains all that is necessary to grasp the main idea contained in the Matthean parallels; for 'though not having moisture' gives the reason for the withering in a neat phrase, and 'growing up with it', συμφυεῖσαι, is a clarification of Matthew's (and Mark's) ἀνέβησαν.

4) There are in this parable no specially vivid details of Mark, although there are some secondary additions, καὶ καρπὸν οὐκ ἔδωκεν, v. 7, and ἀναβαίνοντα καὶ αὐξανόμενα καὶ ἔφερεν in v. 8. This is hardly surprising since this parable has been shown by Jeremias and others to be the thinking of Jesus himself at its deepest and most creative level, and so hardly capable of addition.

5) For the above reasons there are not many examples of Mark's habit of conflating in this unit; his σπεῖραι v. 2, is one.

6) Far more noteworthy is the way in which Mark, instead of following Luke's literary paraphrases, returns always to the actual words of Matthew, just as if they were the form of the story that he himself had always used.

This comparison suggests that far from supporting Luke's editorial 'improvements' to the story, Mark in all respects prefers the version that he found in Matthew.

§7 HEROD'S INTEREST IN JESUS
(Mt 14:1-2 = Lk 9:7-9 = Mk 6:14-16 : BO 159)

Mt 14:1-2	Lk 9:7-9	Mk 6:14-16
¹ Ἐν ἐκείνῳ τῷ καιρῷ ἤκουσεν Ἡρῴδης ὁ τετραάρχης τὴν ἀκοὴν Ἰησοῦ,	⁷ Ἤκουσεν δὲ Ἡρῴδης ὁ τετραάρχης τὰ γινόμενα πάντα,	¹⁴ Καὶ ἤκουσεν ὁ βασιλεὺς Ἡρῴδης, φανερὸν γὰρ ἐγένετο τὸ ὄνομα αὐτοῦ,
(see v. 2 below)	καὶ διηπόρει διὰ τὸ λέγεσθαι ὑπό τινων ὅτι Ἰωάννης ἠγέρθη ἐκ νεκρῶν,	καὶ ἔλεγον ὅτι Ἰωάννης ὁ βαπτίζων ἐγήγερται ἐκ νεκρῶν καὶ διὰ τοῦτο ἐνεργοῦσιν αἱ δυνάμεις ἐν αὐτῷ.
(cf. 16:13-14)	⁸ ὑπό τινων δὲ ὅτι Ἠλίας ἐφάνη, ἄλλων δὲ ὅτι προφήτης τις τῶν ἀρχαίων ἀνέστη.	¹⁵ ἄλλοι δὲ ἔλεγον ὅτι Ἠλίας ἐστίν· ἄλλοι δὲ ἔλεγον ὅτι προφήτης ὡς εἷς τῶν προφητῶν.
² καὶ εἶπεν τοῖς παισὶν αὐτοῦ· οὗτός ἐστιν Ἰωάννης ὁ βαπτιστής·	⁹ εἶπεν δὲ Ἡρῴδης· Ἰωάννην ἐγὼ ἀπεκεφάλισα·	¹⁶ ἀκούσας δὲ ὁ Ἡρῴδης ἔλεγεν· ὃν ἐγὼ ἀπεκεφάλισα Ἰωάννην, οὗτος ἠγέρθη.
αὐτὸς ἠγέρθη ἀπὸ τῶν νεκρῶν, καὶ διὰ τοῦτο αἱ δυνάμεις ἐνεργοῦσιν ἐν αὐτῷ.	τίς δέ ἐστιν οὗτος περὶ οὗ ἀκούω τοιαῦτα; καὶ ἐζήτει ἰδεῖν αὐτόν.	

1) Here again Matthew has 34 words, Luke has 51, Mark has 54.
2) In both Luke and Mark this unit follows on immediately after the initiative of Jesus in sending out the Twelve as itinerant preachers in the dominions of Herod, and no special introduction to the story is required.

3) Luke indeed contains everything that Matthew has, and we have a straightforward instance of how he develops and expands the narrative of Matthew to make things clearer for his readers. For Matthew simply speaks of 'the report about Jesus' without telling us in what this report consists (though he does so later in Mt 16:13-14); and he makes Herod to comment to his courtiers that the extraordinary prodigies of Jesus would seem to indicate that John whom he had beheaded had come to life again.

Luke however expands Matthew's 'the report about Jesus' and tells his readers what these rumours were, vv. 7-8. Luke thought his readers would have a problem with Matthew's v. 2, where Herod declares categorically to his courtiers that 'Jesus is surely John the Baptist risen from the dead — how else could this man work such miracles!' Luke of course realised that Herod was partly puzzled and partly jesting, not understanding why he had failed to quell the movement initiated by John. But Luke feared that his readers might not grasp that Herod was only making a crude joke at the expense of the martyred John and might think that Herod was serious about the possibility of reincarnation. Lest therefore a literal-minded Gentile reader or hearer might be misled into thinking that Jesus could be the reincarnation of John, Luke re-words Herod's utterance into: 'John I beheaded; but who is this about whom I hear such things?'

4) Mark follows the line of Luke in recounting this unit. He adds however the clause, $\varphi\alpha\nu\epsilon\rho\grave{o}\nu$ $\gamma\grave{\alpha}\rho$ $\dot{\epsilon}\gamma\acute{\epsilon}\nu\epsilon\tau o$ $\tau\grave{o}$ $\check{o}\nu o\mu\alpha$ $\alpha\dot{v}\tau o\hat{v}$, v. 14, which reads very much like the comment of one who had been an eye-witness, or at least had known an eye-witness, of these events. Mark however omits Luke's two glosses, $\kappa\alpha\grave{\imath}$ $\delta\iota\eta\pi\acute{o}\rho\epsilon\iota$, 'and he was puzzled', and also the words Luke attributed to Herod: $\tau\acute{\iota}\varsigma$ $\delta\grave{\epsilon}$ $\dot{\epsilon}\sigma\tau\iota\nu$ $o\hat{v}\tau o\varsigma$ $\pi\epsilon\rho\grave{\iota}$ $o\hat{v}$ $\dot{\alpha}\kappa o\acute{v}\omega$ $\tau o\iota\alpha\hat{v}\tau\alpha$; 'who is this about whom I hear such things?'

5) Mark then incorporates into his description of the rumours about Jesus the second half of Herod's verdict as found in Matthew 14:2b: $\kappa\alpha\grave{\imath}$ $\check{\epsilon}\lambda\epsilon\gamma o\nu$ $\check{o}\tau\iota$ $\,{}^{\backprime}\mathrm{I}\omega\acute{\alpha}\nu\nu\eta\varsigma$ $\dot{o}$ $\beta\alpha\pi\tau\acute{\iota}\zeta\omega\nu$ $\dot{\epsilon}\gamma\acute{\eta}\gamma\epsilon\rho\tau\alpha\iota$ $\dot{\epsilon}\kappa$ $\nu\epsilon\kappa\rho\hat{\omega}\nu$, $\kappa\alpha\grave{\imath}$ $\delta\iota\grave{\alpha}$ $\tau o\hat{v}\tau o$ $\dot{\epsilon}\nu\epsilon\rho\gamma o\hat{v}\sigma\iota\nu$ $\alpha\grave{\iota}$ $\delta\nu\nu\acute{\alpha}\mu\epsilon\iota\varsigma$ $\dot{\epsilon}\nu$ $\alpha\dot{v}\tau\hat{\omega}$. But of course having done so, he quickly runs out of words when he comes to his final statement of what Herod actually said. Mark is therefore driven to an abrupt and lame conclusion, and one that is grammatically incomplete, namely, ' . . $\check{o}\nu$ $\dot{\epsilon}\gamma\grave{\omega}$ $\dot{\alpha}\pi\epsilon\kappa\epsilon\varphi\acute{\alpha}\lambda\iota\sigma\alpha$ $\,{}^{\backprime}\mathrm{I}\omega\acute{\alpha}\nu\nu\eta\nu$, $o\hat{v}\tau o\varsigma$ $\dot{\eta}\gamma\acute{\epsilon}\rho\theta\eta$, '. . . whom I beheaded John, this man has been raised'. *The text of Mark only makes proper sense if it is read with both Matthew and Luke before our eyes,* i. e. in the light of Matthew's 'This is John the Baptist; this one has been raised from the dead', and of Luke's 'John I beheaded; but who is this. . .?' Mark has in fact lamely put together parts of both sentences, without properly

changing the grammatical structure; and hence his incoherency. He is surely reporting direct speech, for this explains the discrepancy. In any case it is a striking example of a less successful conflation by Mark.

The interested reader may care to compare our exegesis with that of R. L. Lindsey who thinks he sees in this pericope firm proof of Mark's dependence on Luke. He is surely right in this conclusion, in spite of the fact that he has not fully understood the literary relationships; for he failed to realise that Luke had perfectly understood Matthew, and had then proceeded in the light of his own editorial principles to modify the story. Lindsey is also surely right about Mark's peculiar infelicity in this particular passage.[71]

§8 THE LAWYER'S QUESTION (The Great Commandment)
(Mt 22:34-40 = Lk 10:25-28 = Mk 12:28-34: BO 211, 308)
(Greek synopsis to be found on pp. 106-108)

1) Here again the word count gives Matthew 69, Luke 72, Mark 147.

2) The setting of this unit raises some very interesting problems, which it is necessary to describe in some detail.

Firstly, we note that Mt 22:33, which describes the amazement of the crowds at the way in which Jesus answered the Sadduccees' Question about the Resurrection, is paralleled in Lk 20:39, though not closely in actual wording; 'And certain of the Scribes said, Teacher, you have spoken well' (διδάσκαλε, καλῶς εἶπας); but Mark does not parallel it, though he has an echo at Mk 12:37b. Then there immediately follows in Matthew and Mark the story of the Lawyer's Question, which however has been transferred by Luke to his Central Section. Matthew and Mark have the same unit-sequence, but not so Luke. Thus we have the following scheme:

Q. about the Resurrection	Mt 22:23-33 =	Lk 20:27-40 =	Mk 12:18-27
The Lawyer's Question	22:34-40 =	*10:25-28* =	12:28-34
Jesus' Q. about David's Son	22:41-46 =	20:41-44 =	12:35-37

Before we discuss the reason for this dislocation, we have first to consider some of the consequences of the dislocation itself. For although Luke has omitted this unit from his Main Sequence, his v. 40, 'And they no longer therefore dared to question him about anything' precedes his next unit, David's Son. This v. 40 is actually parallel to Matthew's v. 46, which is placed after the David's Son unit; for the unit that Luke transfers to the Central Section, the Lawyer's Question, is the last question anyone dared to ask him in the Triple Tradition. *But Mark shows that he knows what Luke has done* because he too follows

The Lawyer's Question (BO 211, 308)

Mt 22:33-40	Lk 20:39, 40	Luke (C/S) 10:25-29	Mk 12:28-34 [cf. 12:37b]
33 καὶ ἀκούσαντες οἱ ὄχλοι ἐξεπλήσσοντο ἐπὶ τῇ διδαχῇ αὐτοῦ. 34 οἱ δὲ Φαρισαῖοι ἀκούσαντες ὅτι ἐφίμωσεν τοὺς Σαδδουκαίους συνήχθησαν ἐπὶ τὸ αὐτό, 35 καὶ ἐπηρώτησεν εἷς ἐξ αὐτῶν νομικὸς	39 ἀποκριθέντες δέ τινες τῶν γραμματέων εἶπαν· διδάσκαλε, καλῶς εἶπας.		*(cf. 12:28, 32)*
		25 καὶ ἰδοὺ νομικός τις ἀνέστη	28 Καὶ προσελθὼν εἷς τῶν γραμματέων ἀκούσας αὐτῶν συζητούντων εἰδὼς ὅτι
πειράζων αὐτόν·		ἐκπειράζων αὐτὸν λέγων·	καλῶς ἀπεκρίθη αὐτοῖς, ἐπηρώτησεν αὐτόν·
36 διδάσκαλε, ποία ἐντολὴ μεγάλη ἐν τῷ νόμῳ; 37 ὁ δὲ ἔφη αὐτῷ·		διδάσκαλε, τί ποιήσας ζωὴν αἰώνιον κληρονομήσω; 26 ὁ δὲ εἶπεν πρὸς αὐτόν·	ποία ἐστὶν ἐντολὴ πρώτη πάντων; 29 ἀπεκρίθη ὁ Ἰησοῦς ὅτι πρώτη ἐστίν· ἄκουε, Ἰσραήλ, κύριος ὁ θεὸς ἡμῶν κύριος εἷς ἐστιν, 30 καὶ ἀγαπήσεις κύριον τὸν θεόν σου
ἀγαπήσεις κύριον τὸν θεόν σου			

Mt 22:33-40	Lk 20:39, 40	Luke (C/S) 10:25-29	Mk 12:28-34
ἐν ὅλῃ τῇ καρδίᾳ σου καὶ ἐν ὅλῃ τῇ ψυχῇ σου καὶ ἐν ὅλῃ τῇ διανοίᾳ σου		(cf. 10:27)	ἐξ ὅλης τῆς καρδίας σου καὶ ἐξ ὅλης τῆς ψυχῆς σου καὶ ἐξ ὅλης τῆς διανοίας σου καὶ ἐξ ὅλης τῆς ἰσχύος σου.
38 αὕτη ἐστὶν ἡ μεγάλη καὶ πρώτη ἐντολή. 39 δευτέρα ὁμοία αὐτῇ· ἀγαπήσεις τὸν πλησίον σου ὡς σεαυτόν. 40 ἐν ταύταις ταῖς δυσὶν ἐντολαῖς ὅλος ὁ νόμος κρέμαται καὶ οἱ προφῆται.			31 δευτέρα αὕτη, ἀγαπήσεις τὸν πλησίον σου ὡς σεαυτόν. μείζων τούτων ἄλλη ἐντολὴ οὐκ ἔστιν.
		ἐν τῷ νόμῳ τί γέγραπται; πῶς ἀναγινώσκεις; 27 ὁ δὲ ἀποκριθεὶς εἶπεν·	32 καὶ εἶπεν αὐτῷ ὁ γραμματεύς· καλῶς, διδάσκαλε, ἐπ' ἀληθείας εἶπες ὅτι εἷς ἐστιν, καὶ οὐκ ἔστιν ἄλλος πλὴν αὐτοῦ· 33 καὶ τὸ ἀγαπᾶν αὐτὸν
	(cf. v. 39 above)	ἀγαπήσεις κύριον τὸν θεόν σου	

Mt 22:33-40	Lk 20:39, 40	Luke (C/S) 10:25-29	Mk 12:28-34
		ἐξ ὅλης τῆς καρδίας σου καὶ ἐν ὅλῃ τῇ ψυχῇ σου καὶ ἐν ὅλῃ τῇ ἰσχύϊ σου καὶ ἐν ὅλῃ τῇ διανοίᾳ σου, καὶ τὸν πλησίον σου ὡς σεαυτόν.	ἐξ ὅλης τῆς καρδίας καὶ ἐξ ὅλης τῆς συνέσεως καὶ ἐξ ὅλης τῆς ἰσχύος· καὶ τὸ ἀγαπᾶν τὸν πλησίον ὡς ἑαυτὸν περισσότερόν ἐστιν πάντων τῶν ὁλοκαυτωμάτων καὶ θυσιῶν. ³⁴ καὶ ὁ Ἰησοῦς, ἰδὼν αὐτὸν ὅτι νουνεχῶς ἀπεκρίθη, εἶπεν αὐτῷ·
		²⁸ εἶπεν δὲ αὐτῷ· ὀρθῶς ἀπεκρίθης· τοῦτο ποίει καὶ ζήσῃ.	
		²⁹ ὁ δὲ θέλων δικαιῶσαι ἑαυτὸν εἶπεν πρὸς τὸν Ἰησοῦν· Καὶ τίς ἐστίν μου πλησίον;	οὐ μακρὰν εἶ ἀπὸ τῆς βασιλείας τοῦ θεοῦ.
(cf. 22:46)	(20:40) Οὐκέτι γὰρ ἐτόλμων ἐπερωτᾶν αὐτὸν οὐδέν.		καὶ οὐδεὶς οὐκέτι ἐτόλμα αὐτὸν ἐπερωτῆσαι.

Luke in putting it in front of instead of after the David's Son unit. See my Greek parallel text.

3) This unit is exceptional in that Luke does not contain everything that Matthew has. Far from it. For if we assume that the complete story (a + b) is found in Mark, then Matthew contains part (a) and Luke has part (b). And there is moreover a severe discrepancy between the Matthean and the Lukan version. But we have already seen above when discussing the relations of Luke with Matthew that when Luke finds that his own source has a different content from Matthew's, he carefully avoids juxtaposing the two versions, but transfers his own to another sequence. In this particular instance, he has transferred his own version of this unit to his Central Section. (Cf. his treatment of his Genealogy, the Call of the Four Fishermen, the Nazareth Visit.) But Luke had a further reason for the transfer in this case, for he wished to illustrate Jesus' teaching on the importance of loving one's neighbour by the Parable of the Good Samaritan. It was not possible to insert this parable into the Main Sequence of his Gospel narrative without disrupting its flow; yet at the same time his own version (b) of the story was an admirable introduction to the Parable. Hence its transfer, while leaving a vestige of the excision by the juxtaposition of his v. 39 and v. 40.

4) Mark as often decides to follow the sequence of Matthew, but he also realises what Luke has done and the reason why he has done it. For he takes Luke's part (b) and stitches it onto Matthew's part (a) in a manner that reconciles the discrepancy between them. For whereas in Matthew Jesus himself announces that the two vital commandments of the Law are Love of God and Love of one's neighbour, in Luke the credit of declaring this new commandment is given to the Scribe. But since what Jesus said was something altogether new in the history of Jewish theology, it was impossible that Luke could be right in attributing it to the insight of the Scribe. So Mark by re-affirming for us that Jesus himself made the pronouncement, and that the Scribe both welcomed it and underlined it, reconciles the two narratives.[72] This is perhaps the most remarkable example of Mark's tendency to conflate and harmonise the narratives of Luke and Matthew. We see that Matthew is solely concerned with recording the centrality in Jesus' teaching of his dictum that love of God and love of one's neighbour are equally important. Luke on the other hand is interested in what love of one's neighbour means in ordinary Christian life. Mark is concerned to smoothe out the problem that Luke's concern has created and to 'put the record straight'.

CHAPTER TWELVE

THE MARKAN OMISSIONS

§1 THE OMISSIONS NEED NOT BE A SIGN OF IGNORANCE

The Marcan Omissions of material found in Luke and Matthew are still considered by most critics to be the major stumbling-block to the Priority of Matthew. For it is correctly argued that in general if one document is indebted to another the earlier in date will be the shorter; and so, since Mark is shorter over-all than either Luke or Matthew, it seems more likely to be the earlier. And this probability seems to be greatly reinforced by his undoubtedly vivid, unlettered and colloquial style. But this argument leaves out of account the fact that if one considers just the pericope-units that Mark actually contains, then by comparison Matthew's are the shortest, Luke's are next in order of length, and Mark's are always the longest. And this would favour the supposition that Mark is later than the other two. To put the argument another way, if the original core of the Gospel Message was contained in the 'Triple Tradition' units (although admittedly Mark has them in the longest form), then the additional material about Jesus' Birth and Resurrection appearances found in Luke and Matthew would seem to belong to a later and more developed stage of the tradition. This hypothesis is not unreasonable in itself, other things being equal. But if good reasons are forthcoming for Mark's Omissions, then at once the balance of the argument changes in favour of Mark being the latest of the three.

Let us then consider in turn the major omissions, in the light of what we have learnt from our examination of the units where Mark is parallel to Luke and Matthew. For here alone can we find solid arguments that are not based on a priori considerations. But before we go into detail, there are three preliminary observations to be made:

1. Inspection shows that Mark omits all those units of Luke and Matthew that he could not conflate, but could only juxtapose. Or to put it the other way round, he was only concerned to narrate those episodes of Luke and Matthew that are capable of conflation or harmonisation.

2. If Mark's purpose was to harmonise, and to conflate, then we must expect many omissions.

3. If would seem to be a sound principle that once any Gospel statement or story had appeared in a Gospel that had won acceptance by the Church in general, it did not necessarily have to be repeated in any succeeding Gospel account, unless there happened to be some special reason for doing so.[73]

Thus the Gospel of John, which almost all agree is subsequent to the Synoptics, does not attempt to supply information already accessible in them for the most part. And if Mark were to be subsequent to Luke or Matthew, the same reasoning could apply. There might well be good reasons, of which we are not yet fully aware, why Mark should have made his omissions. Certainly his omissions can only be understood in the total context of the Gospel tradition, and not on the basis of superficial considerations.

§2 THE NATIVITY AND RESURRECTION NARRATIVES, AND THE GENEALOGIES.

There are really two questions here: 1) why did Luke not copy or conflate Matthew, and 2) why did Mark omit altogether?

Let us first take the *Nativity Narratives*. As regards 1) it is to be noted that Matthew and Luke each approaches the origins of Jesus from diverse standpoints. In a brilliant article entitled 'Quis et Unde?' Krister Stendahl (see Bibliog.) explains that Matthew's account is purely apologetical, aiming to destroy two calumnies current in the primitive Palestinian Church milieu about Jesus' origin. Matthew is not really giving us a Birth Narrative, but only showing that in the first place Jesus was not illegitimate but conceived by the Holy Spirit and the true Son of David by legal adoption by Joseph, and secondly, that Jesus' being a Nazarene did not disqualify him from being the Christ. These issues were of burning interest to Palestinian Jews in the first years of Christianity but not to Luke's Gentile readers and hearers. And this explains why Luke supplies them instead with a detailed account of Jesus' conception and birth.

But why did Mark not mention either? Firstly because the witness of Mark's Gospel began only at the Baptism of John and ended at the Discovery of the Empty Tomb; and secondly, because the respective narratives are not conflatable and can only be juxtaposed. Mark had then to choose between omission and juxtaposition; and very reasonably he chose omission, since no useful purpose would be served by juxtaposing them. Indeed, to do so would cause far more worries than omitting them; and so he left each in its own Gospel setting, which best indicates the different view-points of the evangelists to their Christian congregations.

As regards the respective *Resurrection Narratives*.

As to question 1), Matthew is concerned to establish that Jesus had risen physically (cf. 28:9), and that in accordance with his own prophecy he had appeared to the Eleven on a mountain in Galilee and confirmed that they were to preach his message to the whole world and that he would be with them until the End of the Age. Matthew's risen appearances are above all theological. Luke, on the other hand, presupposes the Matthean account, with which he agrees only as far as 24:11 (= Mt 28:1-10). The Resurrection appearances he then relates are diverse but complementary to Matthew's. On the Road to Emmaus and his Ascension narrative he is concerned with the physical nature of the Resurrection Body of Christ; and in his account of the appearance of Jesus to the Eleven in Jerusalem he emphasises the continuity between the Old and New Testament dispensations and develops the teaching of Mt 28: 16-20. In short, Luke's resurrection account is not conflatable with Matthew's.

Now Mark's own account of the Discovery of the Empty Tomb and its significance ends at 16:8 (= Mt 28:10 = Lk 24:1-11). Here again Mark's narrative stops exactly at the point where Luke and Matthew are no longer conflatable.

Finally, as regards the Genealogies, these again cannot be conflated or harmonised, and hence are wisely omitted by Mark. They are diverse because each evangelist approached this history of Jesus from his own standpoint; the result cannot be harmonised and the reason for their diversity can only be apprehended by study of each Gospel separately. No one but a pedant would seriously think of putting them side by side in a work meant to be read aloud to the faithful in the Christian assembly.

§3 THE OMISSION OF LUKE 6:20–8:3.

As regards the Great Sermon, there are many who would argue with L. Vaganay[74] that Mark knew of its existence and deliberately left it out. What is certain is that it was not possible to conflate the Sermon on the Mount with the Sermon on the Plain, especially the Lukan and Matthean Beatitudes. Hence neither features in Mark.

The omission of the whole of Lk 7:1–8:3 appears to provide an exception to the rule we have noted that Mark conflates all the story units where Matthew and Luke run parallel; the Centurion's Slave is the chief exception. Mark's omission of the whole block of Lk 6:20–8:3

may however have some significance; here is the list of the units involved:

	Lk	Mt
The Sermon on the Plain	6:20-49	(5–7)
The Centurion's Slave	7:1-10	8:5-13
Raising of Widow's Son	7:11-17	—
John's Envoys	7:18-23	11:2-6
Jesus praises John	7:24-35	11:7-19
Jesus anointed by a Woman	7:36-50	—
The Ministering Women	8:1-3	—

What we are really looking for is a reason why Mark should in this place pass over the Centurion's Slave and to a lesser degree the two anecdotes about John (for Mark elsewhere shows knowledge of the Baptist's special position, see 1:2ff). We are going to suggest that the whole block is omitted deliberately, and not merely the Great Sermon. And indeed all we need to show is that Mark's omissions here are not unreasonable, according to the Griesbach Hypothesis.

When Mark gets to his 3:19, he notes that Luke has quarried Matthean units down as far as Mt 12:16, i. e. beyond the point where he tells of John's Envoys. We know that Mark has noted this fact because he follows Luke in transferring Mt 12:15-16 back to the place parallel to Luke, i. e. Mk 3:7, 10, 12 = Lk 6:17-18 = Mt 12:15-16 (cf. BO 57, 137).

At this point Mark is faced with the problem of either taking up The Centurion's Slave unit and the two units on John the Baptist and finding room for them after his 6:19, or of following Matthew from 12:(17-22) 23 onwards since Luke breaks off from him at this point. In fact he follows Matthew, which is much easier for him than getting involved in the shuffling of unit-sequences in the manner of Luke. It is true of course that in doing so he omits the Centurion's Slave unit, where Luke had added interesting detail, but to insert it in this case would mean going out of his way. Mark therefore, having followed Luke in giving his list of the Twelve, continues to follow Matthew from the point at which Luke leaves off, and gives the Jesus and Beezelbul units in Matthew's sequence, Mt 12:22-32 = Mk 3:22-30.

Therefore since our hypothesis assumes that Mark continually follows Matthew and/or Luke, since he has both before his eyes, we find here a reasonable explanation of Mark's Great Omission, by which he leaps over the whole block of 6:20–8:3 in order to rejoin the sequence of Matthew, which Luke has temporarily deserted. By doing so Mark incidentally brings back into the main narrative the Beezebul unit which

Luke has relegated to his Central Section.

Mark's omission can therefore be seen to be reasonable and consistent, given his constant preoccupation to follow the sequence of both Matthew and Luke as closely as possible. For once in a way, then, he omits to support Luke's version of three Matthean units, for he is in no way a pedant.

§4 THE OMISSION OF THE CENTRAL SECTION : 9:52–18:14.

Mark omits the whole Central Section (9:52–18:14), that is to say, nearly one third of the whole Gospel of Luke. This is generally agreed by the commentators, for Mark never quotes any material from it, except in those places where there is also a Matthean parallel from which the quotation seems to be taken. This Central Section is, as we have seen, an entirely Lukan editorial construction, and it is another distinctive feature of Mark that he omits all Lukan reconstructions and glosses; see §5 below.

§5 MARKAN OMISSIONS OF LUKAN GLOSSES ON MATTHEW.

That is to say, wherever Luke offers an explanatory comment on any statement in a Matthean unit (as opposed to the furnishing of additional details), Mark omits. The following cases are offered as examples of such omissions:

Mark omits Lk 3:22, σωματικῷ εἴδει
          5:17c, καὶ δύναμις κυρίου ἦν εἰς τὸ ἰᾶσθαι αὐτόν
          22:3a, Εἰσῆλθεν δὲ σατανᾶς εἰς Ἰούδαν
          22:45, ἀπὸ τῆς λύπης
          23:45, τοῦ ηλίου ἐκλιπόντος
          9:45b, καὶ ἦν παρακεκαλυμμένον ἀπ' αὐτῶν ἵνα μὴ αἴσθωνται αὐτό.
          6:11 αὐτοὶ δὲ ἐπλήσθησαν ἀνοίας
          8:15 ἐν ὑπομονῇ
          8:18 ὃ δοκεῖ.

CONCLUSION

CONCLUSION

Chapter Thirteen: Summary of the Whole Argument   117
   1. The Argument of Part Three
   2. Summary of the Argument of Part Two and Part Three together

Chapter Fourteen: Matthew, Luke and Mark   120
   1. The Work of Chapman, Butler and Farmer
   2. The Synoptic Nexus

CHAPTER THIRTEEN

SUMMARY OF THE WHOLE ARGUMENT

§1 SUMMARY OF OUR INVESTIGATION INTO THE RELATIONSHIP OF MARK TO LUKE-WITH-MATTHEW.

It is now time to draw together the threads of our investigation. Looking back now over our application of Mark to Luke-with-Matthew, we see that the comparison indicates certain things:

1) *That Mark follows Matthew more perseveringly than he follows Luke.* For we have firstly the 59 unites of complete Triple Tradition unanimity over sequence. We then have 13 units where Mark follows Luke's deviation from Matthew's sequence. But we also have 7 units where Mark follows Matthew's sequence absolutely against Luke, and we have 6 more units where he prefers Matthew's sequence (relatively) to Luke's. There are also 15 units where Mark follows the sequence of Matthew, when Luke is lacking. Whereas there are only 6 units where Mark follows Luke when Matthew is lacking.

There is only one case where Mark follows his own sequence against both Luke and Matthew; and that is in the case of The First Three Days in Jerusalem and the Cleansing of the Temple. Here the text of Mark is to be viewed as correcting the joint sequence of Luke and Matthew, documenting his action with great care.

2) Again, Mark retains the vestiges of the Matthean Discourses in the same sequence and pattern as Luke, but whereas Luke has transferred most of the abstracted material to his Central Section, there is no visible reason for Mark's retention of them, save that he already found them in Luke.

3) Mark's original additional stories are few in number and seem in any case to be prompted by existing Matthean stories that he has omitted; hence it seems clear that Mark had no intention of making an original contribution to the store provided by Matthew and Luke. His aim and purpose in writing must be looked for in another direction.

4) In this investigation, we have found Mark now supporting both Matthew and Luke, now one or the other, always conflating them,

sometimes harmonising them, occasionally 'correcting' Luke's sequence in relation to Matthew's, not infrequently making the focus on the situation more precise in detail than in Luke. Among such clarifying details it is possible to single out such phrases as *'Talitha koum'* 5:41, ὡς δισχίλιοι (swine) 5:13, καθαρίζων πάντα τὰ βρώματα 7:19.

5) Supporting the theory of harmonisation is the evidence drawn from the Minor Agreements, from the Joint Omissions of Luke and Matthew of words and phrases found in Mark and from Mark's Duplicate Expressions.

6) And as regards the Omissions of Mark, the difficulty arising from these is seen to vanish once it is realised that Mark is neither the source of Luke or Matthew, nor a rival to them, but is concerned with harmonising them.

7) *Mark is concerned to conflate what is conflatable in the two traditions.* What is not conflatable, is guaranteed by the success of conflating what *is* conflatable. And therefore, in the existing context, the omissions are not an argument against Mark knowing Luke and Matthew.

8) It cannot be denied that the convergence of all these different lines of approach is not merely compatible with, but also strongly urges, what imposed itself on Griesbach, namely, that Mark had both Matthew and Luke before his eyes when he composed his Gospel.

§2 SUMMARY OF THE COMBINED ARGUMENT OF PART TWO AND PART THREE.

Given then our presuppositions, which are legitimate since they have not been found to conflict with the evidence of the Gospel text, we have been able to conclude:

1) that Luke's dismemberment and re-shaping of Matthew can be seen to have been done according to a rational plan, a plan —
   a) that respected the basic sequence of Matthew,
   b) that made one change of structure — the switch of the Parables' Discourse,
   c) that made a number of changes of sequence that concerned the ministry in Galilee either before the Great Sermon or between the Great Sermon and the Sending Out of the Twelve,[75]
   d) that transferred the greater part of the material found in the Matthean Discourses to his newly created Central Section, where it is often found illustrated by special anecdotes,

e) that omitted or altered certain things likely to offend the susceptibilities of Gentile Christians,
f) that retained almost everything else of Matthew,
g) that, in order to make room for additional material, omitted some Matthean doublets, often making substitutions,
h) that allowed him to add here and there some background material and some explanatory glosses, which would make certain pericopies more intelligible to future readers and listeners.

2) When Luke, a highly sophisticated literary product, is compared with Matthew (also highly sophisticated in its own way), it is seen to be a re-presentation of the Gospel Message directed towards the Greek Gentile converts rather than to the Jewish Christians of Palestine. This difference of orientation is accentuated by the great quantity of new material introduced by Luke into each of the units of the 'Triple Tradition', units which as a group offer a complete summary of the life and teaching of Jesus from the Baptism of John to the Discovery of the Empty Tomb, units which in their original form certainly pre-date both Matthew and Luke. In other words, in contradistinction to the Gospel Message to the Circumcision, there had come into existence another written Gospel which deliberately addressed itself, in the first place, to Gentile Greek Christians everywhere.

3) And Mark? Mark can be seen in every unit and almost in every line of every unit as harmonising Luke with Matthew. For Mark not only supports the sequence of both as a rule, and then sometimes the one and then the other; but he supports Matthew even more faithfully than Luke, and even occasionally against Luke, and also supplies almost all the important Lukan omissions of Matthew. At the same time, within every unit Mark consistently pursues his role as conflator, harmoniser, explicator and critic; and in one instance he will give detailed reasons for diverging from both (The Cleansing of the Temple).

On the assumption of Matthean priority, the literary relationships between the three Gospels can be readily understood in terms of simple editorial activity on the part of the evangelists Luke and Mark. This is not to deny that the 'story-units' and the 'sayings' had a history of their own prior to their inclusion in the Gospels, nor that the evangelists had not over-riding theological purposes that governed their selection and adaptation of the stories they found in the oral tradition. The facts indicate that they acted in this way; why they did so is a question yet to be discussed.

CHAPTER FOURTEEN

MATTHEW, LUKE AND MARK

§1 THE WORK OF CHAPMAN, BUTLER AND FARMER

All past attempts to replace the Markan Priority Theory have failed to convince biblical scholars either because in some way they did not establish the real relationships between Luke and Matthew and between Mark and Luke-with-Matthew, or because they omitted to offer a more plausible alternative.

Chapman failed because the climate of opinion was too hostile for a posthumous work that advocated a return to the Augustinian Hypothesis and also failed to perceive Mark's true relationship to Luke.

Butler failed to win much support for the same reasons, though he did in fact succeed in destroying the major arguments for the existence of 'Q'.

Farmer then introduced a new element, the Griesbach Hypothesis, and finally succeeded in undermining the arguments upon which Streeter had reared his Four-Document Hypothesis. But he too failed to win general support, partly because his critics did not take his arguments seriously enough, and partly because at that time he did not attempt to offer an adequate theory of origins to replace the theory whose foundations he had destroyed.

Nevertheless the work of each of these scholars marked a progressive development in the evolution of a more realistic theory of synoptic origins; and the present work could not have been begun without reliance on the solid foundations already laid in their writings. Their labours have in fact opened the way for the writing of the present book.

§2 THE SYNOPTIC NEXUS

What exactly then has now been established in Part One, Two and Three? Quite simply this: there now exists a scientific and reasonable alternative to the consensus view of the literary relationships between the Synoptic Gospels. This alternative solution is based on two assumptions that are in themselves a priori reasonable, namely, that

Greek Matthew could have been the first Gospel to appear, and that Mark was not in existence when the final redactor of Luke decided to re-interpret the Gospel of Matthew in a free yet respectful manner.

In Part Two, solid grounds have been offered for believing that Luke is the result of an intelligent and purposeful dissection of Matthew in order to re-assemble the great bulk of the same material in a somewhat different though similar pattern. In Part Three, further solid grounds have been offered for holding that Mark is the purposeful result of another editor intelligently conflating, harmonising, supporting, and occasionally modifying, the story and sayings units found between the Baptism of John and the Discovery of the Empty Tomb.

In other words, the three Synoptic Gospels can now be seen to have an intelligible literary relationship with one another, and to cohere together without the aid of Mark or any 'Q' source; provided we admit that each also had its own special source or sources, which were in their turn part of the Palestinian oral tradition, i. e. of the original fund of such stories and sayings as existed in Palestine prior to the composition of the first of the Gospels. This literary Nexus between Matthew, Luke and Mark is to be understood as being quite independent of any date that might be credibly assigned to any of them; it simply establishes a mutual, timeless, and immutable literary relationship between the three of them. It is a Nexus that is quite possibly compatible with more than one hypothesis of how the Gospels came into historical existence; but it is not compatible with the existence of 'Q', since Matthew is now established as the principal source for the material common to Luke and Matthew.

This Nexus is, it seems, a solid fact, and a fact that immediately cries out for explanation. This book is however concerned solely with the establishment of the fact, i. e. that this literary Nexus is really there and is clearly discernible in the original texts. To admit its existence is only the first stage in a new quest — a stage that will undoubtedly require further verification from many angles before it can meet with general acceptance. But to explain its existence is quite a different matter.

The next stage of the present inquiry—the second stage—is to take a long cool look at the present results fairly set out in the form of a New Griesbach Synopsis. This will be done in Volume II, which will be the essential companion to the present volume. Thereafter, the scientific foundations of the New Griesbach Hypothesis having been laid, it will then become possible to offer in a third volume measured and credible answers to the two questions with which we still have to contend, namely,

1) Why did Luke treat Matthew in the way we have shown?; and
2) Why did Mark then act as we have seen him?

Publishing problems notwithstanding, it is hoped that these two volumes will follow shortly and thus complete in outline the presentation of the New Griesbach Hypothesis.

FOOTNOTES

FOOTNOTES

CHAPTER ONE

1. H. Palmer, *The Logic of Gospel Criticism*, London, 1968, p. 136; cf. also R. Morgenthaler, *Statistische Synopse*, p. 279 col. A, who writes as follows: 'the fact that redaction-critical research, like synoptic research, has failed to result in a satisfactory consensus concerning the redaction of the single gospels gives pause to think. The lack of consensus in the interpretation of the synoptic redaction is in fact very great' (translated by the present writer). E. P. Sanders (*The Tendencies of the Synoptic Tradition*, Cambridge, 1969) concludes his work with the statement: 'The evidence does not seem to warrant the degree of certainty with which many scholars hold the two-document hypothesis' (p. 278).
2. B. Lonergan, *Method in Theology*, 1972, p. 171.
3. F. Gast has a brief but comprehensive survey of the present state of the Synoptic Problem in his article 'Synoptic Problem' in *The Jerome Biblical Commentary*, 1968, N.T. section art. 40.
4. H. J. Holtzmann, *Die Synoptischen Evangelien, Ihr Ursprung und ihr geschichtlicher Character*, Leipzig, 1863, pp. 63-67. Holtzmann himself never actually used the term 'Q', but referred to the collection of Jesus' Sayings as 'L' for Logia. See also F. Bleek, *An Introduction to the New Testament*, tr. from 2nd ed. by R. Urwick, 2 vols. Edinburgh, 1869-70. §§ 100-102.
5. It seems that nobody today holds the extreme view of the Oral Hypothesis, i. e. that the Gospels are not in direct literary relationship either with each other or with hypothetical earlier documents, but only with primitive circulating oral tradition; but see A. G. de Fonseca *Quaestio Synoptica*, 3rd ed. (P. B. I., Rome, 1952), for a learned defence of a variation of this view. For a moderate view, see X. Léon-Dufour, *The Gospels and the Jesus of History*, Collins, Fontana 1970, pp. 187ff (trans. from Les Evangiles et L'histoire de Jesus, 1963). Riesenfeld and Gerhardsson have put the matter in a nutshell, 'the greatest problem for the Oral Hypothesis is to explain the order of the Triple Tradition' (quoted by A. Gaboury, *Structure des Evangiles*, 1970, pp. 7ff). W. G. Kümmel, in his *Introduction to the New Testament*, English ed. SCM Press 1966 (trans. from 14th revised German edition of 1965) admirably sums up the matter on p. 60: '(The three synoptic Gospels are) to a certain degree fixations of a certain stage of oral tradition. . . but beyond that. . . they are the work of purposive authors who shaped the traditions theologi-

cally'. This well-known work may be said in most ways to be representative of modern German biblical opinion, and for that reason will be quoted again not infrequently. Cf. also R. Bultmann, *The History of the Synoptic Tradition*, English ed. Oxford, 1963.

CHAPTER TWO

6. This chapter is greatly indebted to William R. Farmer's brilliant analysis in *The Synoptic Problem*, 1964, chaps 1–5.
7. Griesbach announced his conversion from the Augustinian sequence in his opusculum, first published in 1789, entitled, *Io. Iac. Griesbachii Theol. D. et Prof. Primar in academia Jenensi commentario Qua Marci Evangelium totum e Matthaei et Lucae commentariis discerptum esse monstratur, scripta nomine Academiae Jenensis.* (All quotations are taken from the edition published at Jena in 1825 by Io. Philippus Gabler.) In this work Griesbach, while continuing to accept the priority of Matthew over Luke and Mark, affirms that Mark 'in conscribendo suo libro ante oculos positum habuisse non solum Mattheum sed et Lucam, et ex his decerpsisse quicquid de rebus gestis, sermonibus et fatis Servatoris memoriae mandaret' (Gabler, ed. p. 365). In Section II of the same work he offers three reasons, and in Section III he answers various objections.
8. This was the effect of F. L. Sieffert's *Über den Ursprung des ersten canonischen Evangeliums, eine kritische Abhandlung*, Königsberg, 1832.
9. See note 4.
10. E.g. F. P. Badham, *St Mark's Indebtedness to St Matthew*, London 1897; E. W. Lummis, *How Luke was Written*, Cambridge, 1915; H. G. Jameson, *The Origin of the Synoptic Gospels*, Oxford, 1922. Both the latter attacked the Two-Document Hypothesis at the sensitive point of the Minor Agreements between Matthew and Luke against Mark, and both were entirely ignored by Streeter when he published his *Four Gospels* in 1924, as Farmer was to point out devastatingly in *The Synoptic Problem*, pp. 152ff.
11. Abbot H. J. Chapman's posthumous *Matthew, Mark and Luke*, London, 1937, was in fact the first challenge to the thesis of Streeter. It failed to make any impression, firstly because it was published posthumously (Chapman had died in 1933); secondly, because the script had been left in an incomplete state at the author's death; and thirdly because it was assumed to be a Roman Catholic apologetical effort rather than a scientific exposition.
12. This short but seminal volume after many years of neglect eventually started a new trend through its influence on Farmer. In French-speaking circles, dissatisfaction with the Two-Document Hypothesis had already shown itself in the work of Père J.-M. Lagrange, in his commentary on Matthew (1923) and on Mark (1929).

13. See *Jésus aux Evangiles* (Donum Coppens), Journées Bibliques, Louvain, 1965, edited by I. de la Potterie, 'Traduction et Rédaction dans les Evangiles synoptiques.'
14. Interesting evidence of this change can be seen by comparing *The Catholic Commentary on Holy Scripture*, 1953, with its second edition in 1969, entitled *A New Catholic Commentary*, edited by R. C. Fuller. In Germany since 1945 the only important scholar to maintain the Priority of Matthew in the tradition of Schlatter has been K. H. Rengstorf.
    The adoption of the Two-Document Hypothesis by the great majority of Catholic scholars in recent years may be regarded as a prime factor in their admission to the international fraternity of New Testament scholars, thereby incidentally providing a convenient basis for ecumenical discussion in the biblical world.
15. For example: 'Les arguments qu'on apporte ne permettent pas de conclure à la priorité de l'un ou de l'autre évangile' wrote A. Gaboury. Unable to base his researches on the existing consensus, he sought a new way by means of his 'péricope-techniques' (*La Structure des Evangiles*, pp. 29-31).
    L. Sabourin quotes a statement by D. Guthrie to the effect that 'no one can deny that the data available for pre-literary or pre-synoptic study are not particularly cogent' and comments that 'in fact they are to be inferred from our Gospel texts usually in line with preconceived theories' (art. 'Recent Gospel Studies', *Bib. Theology Bulletin*, 3 (1973) 309). In the same article, in which he is reviewing the present state of the Synoptic Question as a prelude to a review of Boismard's Synopsis, Vol. II, Sabourin concludes that 'No one is yet authorised to make dogmatic pronouncements regarding the Synoptic Problem', p. 309.
16. See the bibliography for details of their synoptic writings.
17. Walter Wink, reviewing Tome 2 of P. Benoit and M. E. Boismard, *Synopse des Quatres Evangiles en français*, 1972, in the *Catholic Biblical Quarterly* 35 (1973) 223-25, wrote as follows: 'Many are still unaware of this historic significance of W. R. Farmer's *The Synoptic Problem*, 1964. Wholly apart from its positive alternative (the Griesbach Hypothesis *redivivus*), which has commended itself to very few indeed, Farmer's work was important for its negative accomplishment. Quite simply, he demolished the theoretical basis of the two-document hypothesis as definitively formulated by Streeter. To those able to take this event seriously, it became clear that either Farmer's alternative was right or else a new basis would have to be laid for the two-document hypothesis, one far more complex than formerly, able to do justice to all the anomalies previously ignored, especially the so-called Minor Agreements of Matthew and Luke against Mark.' With this verdict Gaboury agrees; for he had pre-

viously written: 'tout l'effort de W. R. Farmer vise à ébranler la foi trop candide en la priorité de Marc. Sur ce point, il faut avouer que le travail de Farmer est une réussite' (*La Structure,* p. 27). However Gaboury asserts that Farmer thinks — wrongly — that 'détruire la priorité de Marc équivaut à affirmer la priorité de Matthieu' (p. 28).

18. Yet the widespread ignorance of the import of the new work on the synoptic question is attested by the fact that a scholar of the eminence of G. Bornkamm can continue to write: 'there are strong arguments for the common assumption of the chronological priority of Mark (Matthew having been previously assumed to be the earliest Gospel)... For the reasons indicated we are no longer justified in speaking of the first plank of the two-source theory — the priority of Mark — as a mere hypotheis. It leaves plenty of questions unanswered. But we need not go into them here, and anyway they represent no serious challenge to the theory as such. Seldom does it happen, as here, that the historian is in the happy position of being able constantly to use as a control an earlier source still extant in a tolerably complete literary form.' This quotation is from Gunther Bornkamm, *The New Testament, A Guide to its Writings,* Fortress Press, Philadelphia, 1973, (itself a translation from *Das Neues Testament. Eine Einfuhrung in seine Schriften in Rahmen des Geschichte des Urchristentums,* 1971, Kreuz-Verlag, Stuttgart). But Bornkamm does not advance a single argument that has not been effectively demolished either by Butler or Farmer. For an excellent survey of recent German work on the Synoptic Gospels, see. J. Rohde, *Rediscovering the Teaching of the Evangelists,* SCM Press, London, 1968.

CHAPTER THREE

19. See *Rediscovering the Teaching of the Evangelists,* English Edition, SCM Press, London, 1968, p. 5: translated from the original *Die Redaktionsgeschichtliche Methode,* 1966.
20. F. H. Woods, 'The Origin and Mutual Relation of the Synoptic Gospels', *Studia Biblica et Ecclesiastica* II (Nov. 1886) 60f.
21. Kümmel, op. cit., p. 43. G.M. Styler agrees that B. C. Butler has succeeded in destroying the argument from Order as a safe argument for the Priority of Mark (cf. Excursus IV, 'The Priority of Mark', p. 224, in C. F. D. Moule, *The Birth of the New Testament,* 2nd ed. 1966). For Streeter had argued, 'Mark is clearly the more primitive, for when for example Matthew leaves the order of Mark, Luke follows Mark; and if it is Luke who leaves the order of Mark, Matthew supports the order of Mark. And on the contrary, there is no case where Matthew and Luke agree against Mark on the point of order', (*The Four Gospels,* 1927, p. 161). Though there may indeed be partial exceptions; yet because he could not personally see any good reason for Mark being the third Gospel, Streeter ignored the fact

that the above phenomenon of order is equally explicable on the Griesbach assumption that Luke in general followed Matthew, but with a number of significant changes of pericope-order which Mark accepted, though in a few cases Mark modifies (or corrects) the order of Luke, and that of Matthew on one occasion too. If the phenomenon can be easily explained on the assumption that Mark came third after the other two, the same assumption also explains why Matthew and Luke never agree against Mark on a point of order. For Mark either agrees with one or the other, or disagrees with one or the other, and never with both at the same time! (The Nazareth Visit, Mk 6:1-6, is hardly an exception).

22. E. P. Sanders, 'The Argument from Order and the Relationship between Matthew and Luke' in *New Test. Stud.* 15, pp. 249-253.
23. W. F. Farmer, *The Synoptic Problem*, pp. 190-191, and n. 16.
24. Kümmel, for example, still claims (op. cit., p. 48) that arguments from style, comparison of language and subject-matter are decisive for Markan priority; cf. also G. M. Styler, op. cit., p. 230. E. P. Sanders (*Tendencies. . .* p. 272) has declared that 'dogmatic statements that a certain characteristic proves a certain passage to be earlier than another are never justified'. And he continues: 'One may only say that the balance of probability is that material richer in detail and direct speech is later' (p. 274). And Mark is the richer in detail and direct speech!
25. See however F. Neirynck's comprehensive list of 'The Duplicate Expressions in the Gospel of Mark' in *Eph. Theol. Lov.* Jan-Mar 1972, pp. 151-209. This material of Neirynck's has recently been published as a separate work, entitled *Duality in Mark*, Leuven, 1972. Neirynck's idea is to offer an alternative explanation of the seeming conflatory tendencies of Mark by suggesting that they are part of Mark's own style, and not due to the influence of Luke and Matthew.
26. 'Minor Agreements' of Matthew and Luke against Mark are found distributed evenly throughout the Gospels. The following is an incomplete list. The Matthean parallel alone is given. Some are found in: Mt. 3:1-6, 7-10, 11-12, 13-17; 4:1-11, 12, 23; 8:1-4, 14-15, 16-17. 23-27, 28-34; 9:1-8, 9-13, 14-17, 18-26; 10:2-4, 14, 26; 11:7-19; 12:1-8, 9-14, 15-16, 46-50; 13:1-2, 3-9, 10-11, 18-23; 14:1-2, 13-21; 16:13-20, 21:24-28; 17:1-9, 14-21, 22-23; 18:1-5; 19:13-15, 16-22, 23-29; 20:17-19, 29-34; 21:1-9, 12-13, 23-27, 33-46; 22:15-22, 23-33, 41-46; 23:1, 5c-7; 24:3-7, 8, 19, 29-33; 26:1-19, 26-29, 30-35, 36-46, 47-56, 57-75; 27:1-2, 11-14, 15-16, 32, 33-44, 54, 55-56, 57-61; 28:1-8.
27. For the treatment of some of these agreements, see B. H. Streeter, *The Four Gospels,* in loc.; and see W. R. Farmer, *The Synoptic Problem,* 1964, pp. 94-177 for the complete refutation of Streeter's presentation; see also N. Turner, 'The Minor Verbal Agreements of

Matthew and Luke against Mark', *Studia Ev. Texte u. Unters.* Band 73, p. 223; cf. also Bibliography for F. Neirynck's full list of these Agreements. It should be noted that Kümmel in his Introduction (op. cit.) does not attempt to deal with the problems created for the Priority of Mark by these agreements and omissions, the reasons being, it seems, that German scholarship has not recently paid much attention to them. (F. R. T. Simpson, 'The Major Agreements of Matthew and Luke against Mark', *N. T. S.* 12 (1965-66) 273-284.)

28. G. M. Styler was reluctantly forced to admit that 'unless we are allowed to appeal to "Q" and say that it is some knowlege of "Q" (i. e. of Matthew's source) which Mark betrays (e. g. in the teaching of the Baptist), Butler's conclusion (the literary indebtedness of Mark to Matthew) does indeed seem to be forced upon us' (op. cit., p. 227). A. M. Farrer wrote: 'To get rid of "Q" as a source of Luke we mere have to make St Luke's use of St Matthew intelligible' ('On Dispensing with 'Q' in *Studies in the Gospels*, ed. Nineham, Oxford 1957, p. 66). Even Kümmel has to admit that there are many unsolved problems connected with the existence of 'Q' (op. cit., pp. 51-58).

29. From *On the Gattung of Mark (and John)* pp. 102-103, quoted by F. Neirynck on p. 69 of *L'Evangile selon Matthieu*, ed. M. Didier, (Duculot, Gembloux 1972), Farmer has written: 'This argument may be formally stated as follows: "It is inconceivable that so many scholars could have been so wrong on such a fundamental point for such a long period of time." This is a powerful argument precisely because it is in practice irrefutable' (*The Synoptic Problem*, p. 195).

30. Further up-to-date information may be found in David Wenham's 1971 Tyndale New Testament Lecture, Cambridge, entitled, 'The Synoptic Problem Revisited', which contains an acute analysis of the weaknesses of the Two-Document Hypothesis, and argues for the priority of Matthew. X. Léon-Dufour's analysis of the Two-Document Hypothesis ('Le Fait synoptique' in *R. Sc. Rel.* 60 (1972) 495-496) is brilliant and his conclusion is worth quoting here: 'Peut-on parler de "deux" sources, lorsqu'on renonce à préciser exactement en quoi elles consistaient; d'un côté un proto-Marc, de l'autre une documentation, tous deux résultant d'une induction à partir des données synoptiques? Osons le dire: quoique apparemment précise, la théorie des Deux-Sources reste dans le vague. Mérite-t-elle dès lors de commander l'exercice de l'exégèse synotique?'

31. Griesbach allows that it is a question that should have an answer, but in fact it would seem that he took no steps to answer it, see *Opus. XXII*, p. 418.

32. W. G. Kümmel (*Introduction* op. cit., p. 39) for instance rejects brusquely the Griesbach Hypothesis as 'assuming too many improbabilities, and failing to recognise the independence of Mark'! From the standpoint of one who accepts the Priority of Mark as an unas-

sailable fact, this seems obvious; but the improbabilities arise just because the Griesbach Hypothesis is always looked at against the background created by the Two-Document Hypothesis. And this is to argue in a circle. If it is a truism to say that the Two-Document Hypothesis denies the independence of Matthew, it is just as much a truism to assert that the Griesbach Hypothesis denies the independence of Mark. All that Kümmel's assertion means is that because the Griesbach Hypothesis is contrary to the Two-Document Hypothesis it must therefore be wrong!

33. Cf. Streeter's sarcastic phrases which have so often withered sensible questionings, 'Only a lunatic would leave out Matthew's account of the Infancy, The Sermon on the Mount, and practically all the Parables, in order to get room for purely verbal expansion of what was retained' (*The Four Gospels*, 1927, impr., p. 158). What Streeter failed to realise was that there could have been (and in fact were) other reasons, most sensible ones, why Mark did precisely that. The narrowness of Streeter's outlook is further shown by his other famous stricture on those who thought otherwise than himself, (see p. 164 of the same volume).

34. A. Jepsen has recently written that although Mark *need* not be later in time (than Matthew) it can be so evaluated; see his article in *Nov. Test.* 14 (1972) 106, 114. Fewer and fewer scholars are today prepared to be dogmatic in their assertion that Matthew could not have been published before 70 A.D. At the conclusion of his important lecture 'Matthew against his Time', given at Los Angeles, 1972, W. F. Davies (Duke Divinity School) said in answer to a question on this point that 'the whole interpretation of Matthew is in the melting pot'. It is very hard indeed to be sure that there is any solid evidence in the Gospel itself against a pre-70 date.

35. The strongest case so far made out against Farmer's thesis was presented by Joseph A. Fitzmyer at the Pittsburgh Festival and printed in *Jesus and Man's Hope*, Part 1, (Pittsburgh Theological Seminary, 1970), in his article: 'On the Gospel of Luke, The Priority of Mark and the "Q" Source in Luke', where Fitzmyer argues:— (1) that Farmer's first argument for Mark being third depends on an argument from order, which Fitzmyer believes to be weak; (2) that Farmer gives no convincing reason why Mark should omit the preaching of the Baptist; (3) from the inconclusive nature of the Christological argument for the primitive character of Mark; and (4) that Farmer's reasons for Mark being third are not convincing. At the same time and in the same volume, David L. Dungan in an extremely penetrating and witty paper (which gave some the impression of 'flippancy'—unjustly), presented the case against the priority of Mark and a case for the priority of Matthew ('On the Gospel of Mark' in *Jesus and Man's Hope*, pp. 51-98.

36. See B. Lonergan, *Insight*, XVII, 3, 'The Truth of Interpretation', for an interesting discussion of principles. In a question of this complexity it is only too easy to overlook possible flaws in one's own method. For instance, the fallacy of regarding the argument from order as decisive for the Priority of Mark, though several times exposed, (e. g. by Jameson, op. cit. above in 1922), was not finally admitted as such until 1957; see Styler's admission in Excursus IV cited previously in Note 17, above; see also Butler's *Originality of St Matthew*, p. 65. Indeed there are still certain circles in which the old argument from Order is trotted out as if nothing had happened, cf. Note 16. Yet strange to relate in this same volume in which he correctly exposed the flaw in the use of the argument from Order, Butler himself overlooked the vital alternative to the Augustinian Hypothesis, when he failed to see that the order: (1) Matthew, (2) Luke, (3) Mark, was feasible, and that he ought not to have ruled it out *a priori*.

CHAPTER FOUR

37. The denial of the existence of 'intermediate documents' is quite compatible with the view that before even the first of the Gospels was composed there were already in existence a number of prepared stories about Jesus, which were the basis of catechetical instruction in the primitive Church. Some of them were *Chreiai*, enshrining the (deeds and) sayings of Jesus and known by heart; others were longer, Extended Chreiai in fact, or *Apomnemoneumata*. These literary forms must have been taken over and used in diverse ways and for diverse theological reasons by each in turn of the synoptic evangelists. The pre-existence of such material is perfectly compatible with the editorial processes envisaged in Category 1).

38. However in his recent book, *Midrash and Lection in Matthew*, 1974, Professor M. D. Goulder has proposed a new theory which, while accepting the priority of Mark, explains Matthew as a Midrash based on Mark and Paul, but with Luke in some way dependent on Matthew — in this way maintaining the priority of Mark without the need for 'Q'. Suffice it to say that according to the principle enunciated in the text above, his theory is next in line for consideration should the Revised Griesbach Hypothesis prove inadequate.

CHAPTER FIVE

39. Griesbach was the first to use the word 'synopsis' in this sense in his edition of 1774. In this synopsis he placed Matthew in the left-hand column, Mark in the middle, and Luke on the right, seemingly because at the date of its original publication in 1774/6 he still thought that Mark was second to Matthew. Surprisingly enough, after he had publicly notified his conversion in 1789 to the belief

that Luke also was prior to Mark, he failed to alter the relative places of the Lukan and Markan columns in later editions. And of course when many years later the era of Markan priority arrived, his original arrangement continued to stand, as it happened incidentally to illustrate very well the theory of Mark as intermediary between Matthew and Luke.

40. The unconscious bias in favour of Markan priority may be noted in the lay-out of most modern synopses; see for example their treatment of Mk 13 as central between Matthew and Luke. Cf. also the Introduction to R. Morgenthaler, *Statistische Synopse,* 1971, part I, section 7. Cf. J. B. Orchard, *On Making a Gospel Synopsis.*
41. The two books are R. O. P. Taylor, *The Groundwork of the Gospels,* Oxford, 1946; and B. Gerhardsson, *Memory and Manuscript,* Uppsala, 1961.
42. It can therefore be no mere coincidence that Justin Martyr (c. 150 A. D.) can refer to the Gospels as 'the *apomnemoneumata* of the Apostles', *Dialogue with Trypho,* 106, 1-3; 103, 8; 81, 4.
43. B. de Solages in his recent book *La Composition des Evangiles,* 1973, has followed the lead of A. Gaboury in examining the pericope order of Matthew and Luke. He began to use this method only after convincing himself of the priority of Mark by the method of comparative literary analysis (cf. his *Synopse grecque, methode nouvelle*, 1959). If he had begun with an independent study of the pericope order, he might well have come to a very different conclusion. See Farmer's critique in *The Synoptic Problem*, pp. 197-8.
44. Unfortunately the efforts of scholars have been concentrated on the second method—the reasons are understandable—to the neglect of the prior method. The absence of such a check on the method of comparative literary analysis has been very serious; for though the latter should in theory have led to a sure and agreed result, it has in fact failed to do so. Thus we find X. Léon-Dufour lamenting, after so much effort by so many scholars 'l'incertitude et l'imprécision des résultats de l'analyse litteraire', *Rev. Scien. Relig.* (1972) 495. Yet it is seldom noted that the real reason for the 'incertitude' could be either an error of method or a fault in fundamental assumptions.
45. The reader might like to have a modern illustration of this process, which may be found in the relationship of the original *Peake's Commentary* (1920) with the first edition of *A Catholic Commentary on Holy Scripture*, ed. J. B. Orchard (1953). When I planned the latter work I took as my pattern Peake's list of contents. That is to say, I wrote down the headings of all his introductory chapters in both the Old and New Testaments sections; I measured the number of columns he had allotted to each article or commentary, and took this as the basis of discussion from which our own editorial board produced the plan for the CCHS as published. Of course we discarded certain titles

as inappropriate for a work *ex professo* setting out the Roman Catholic standpoint—this was before the days of ecumenism—and added in other titles such as 'Replies of the Biblical Commission' and 'Our Lady in the Scriptures', It is probably true to say that there was practically no copying of the content of any of the articles in Peake, for we were setting forth a different Church tradition. Nevertheless there is no doubt at all that the basic pattern of chapters owes a very great deal to Peake's own sequence and plan. That is to say, the General Editor of the CCHS, having Peake before him, took full advantage of his pioneer work, but nonetheless made all the changes he wanted to suit the purpose of the CCHS. The assertion made here is that *mutatis mutandis* it is a reasonable hypothesis that Luke did much the same with Matthew.

CHAPTER SIX

46. This supposition is of course ruled out *a priori*, in the Two-Document Hypothesis, as being impossible. But our contention is that not one conclusive argument has ever been produced to prove the impossibility. It is this possibility that we are now investigating. The procedure now to be followed is based on the following assumptions:

(1) The validity of the Pericope Unit technique for assessing the dependence of the plan or structure of one work on another.

(2) The acceptance of the general opinion that the Gospel of Mark has had no influence on the Central Section of Luke, cf. Hawkins, *Horae Synopticae*, Oxford, 1911, p. 39.

(3) The consensus that Matthew has not borrowed from Luke, cf. G. M. Styler, Excursus IV, in C. F. D. Moule, *The Birth of the New Testament*[2], 1966, p. 225.

(4) That for the purpose of this investigation, it is in order to prescind from the complicated question of the relationship of Matthew and Luke to Mark.

(5) That it is not unreasonable to assume as a working hypothesis that canonical Luke could depend on canonical Matthew. This possibility has never lacked authoritative support, e. g. E. Simons, *Hat der dritte Evangelist den kanonischen Matthäus benützt?*, Bonn, 1880; B. C. Bulter, 'St Luke's Debt to St Matthew', *Harvard Theological Review*, 32 (1939) no. 4; Bishop Cassian, 'Luke after Matthew but before John', *Stud. Ev. Texte u. Unters.*, Band 73, pp. 142-147; R. Morgenthaler, *Statistische Synopse*, 1971, pp. 278 col. B—279 col. A. On the other hand, H. A. Guy, *Exp. Times* 83 (1972) denies the possibility.

47. A. Gaboury (op. cit., p. 10) asks the right basic question: 'La structure de base, s'identifie-t-elle avec une des évangiles, ou avec une évangile anterieure à ceux-ci?', and then unfortunately goes on to give an *a priori* answer which prejudges the issue. For he continues

(op. cit., p. 11): 'Pour expliquer l'ordonnance commune aux synoptiques, il est nécessaire de recourir à une structure de base, c'est-à-dire, à une stade de formation déjà évolue', and goes on to affirm 'la source de base qui est à l'origine du fait synoptique, a été constituée avant les évangiles actuelles.' But in making this vague and dubious affirmation he has answered his fundamental question without offering evidence, and closed the door to any hypothesis other than one of the many forms of Markan priority. Hence he never even refers to the Griesbach Hypothesis, thus ignoring a whole possible new field of research.

48. By the 'main structure' of Luke is meant in fact Lk 1:9–9:51 together with Lk 18:15 to the end of the Gospel. For it is in these parts of Luke that we find a structure almost identical with that of Matthew 1:1–28:20. The main structure of Matthew is seen to be centred around the Six Great Discourses, flanked by the Nativity narrative and other preparatory material on the one side, and the Passion and Resurrection narratives on the other.

49. By 'Units in absolute sequence' is meant those units which are in the same sequence throughout in the Gospel framework; by 'Units in relative sequence' are meant those which retain the same sequential relationship to one another after transfer.

50. Agreed statistics are not possible until there is prior agreement on the actual sub-division of the text into idea-units. These figures are close approximations only.

51. On close inspection the respective Nativity Narratives are in fact found to agree on a number of important points, i.e. that Jesus was begotten by the Virgin Mary through the Holy Spirit, that Joseph her husband was only the putative father of Jesus, and that the family travelled back to Nazareth sometime after the birth of Jesus and settled there. See. P. J. Thompson, 'The Infancy Gospels of St Matthew and St Luke compared', *Texte u. Unters.* Band 73 (1959), pp. 217ff. On the other hand K. Stendahl in 'Quis et Unde' (an article in *Festschrift für J. Jeremias*, 1960) has shown that it is wrong to speak of the Birth material in Matthew and Luke as 'alternative Birth narratives'. They are nothing of the sort. Mt 1 describes the fact of Jesus having no earthly father and his official adoption by Joseph into the Davidic line as a Davidic child. Matthew 2 explains how it came to pass that the Messiah came from Nazareth. That is to say, Matthew 1–2 are entirely apologetical in purpose. Hence the Lukan narrative can only be complementary, not alternative.

CHAPTER SEVEN

52. Some idea of the convergence of units between Lk 4:44–6:19 as compared with the dispersal of the same between Mt 4:23–12:16 may be realised from the numbering of the units in KA. Here

Lk 4:44–6:19 are §§40-50, while Mt 4:23–12:16 are within the span of §§40-113.
53. When we speak about Luke having a 'chronological' reason for a change, we are not in any way precluding that he may well have had other reasons as well, e. g. theological ones. It is simply that in a particular context, the chronological reason seems to have been an important factor also.
54. It is worth noting that Luke marks each block of these transfers by an editorial prefacing phrase, which indicates the dislocation. For after Lk 4:44 (a general reference to the First Preaching Tour), he inserts a unit parenthetically, namely The Miraculous Catch 5:1-11. Its parenthetical character is shewn by its inclusion between 5:1a (ἐγένετο δὲ ἐν τῷ τὸν ὄχλον κτλ) and 5:12a (καὶ ἐγένετο κτλ) Thereby Luke is informing us that The Miraculous Catch (i. e. The Call of the Four) preceded by an unspecified period the First Preaching Tour (5:12ff) in which they followed Jesus. In recording this Tour Luke continues to give each single unit or block of units transferred its own prefacing phrase, which acts as a connecting link. Thus 5:12-16 (= Mt 8:1-4), The Cleansing of the Leper, found in a different sequence in Matthew, is prefaced in Luke by καὶ ἐγένετο ἐν τῷ εἶναι ἐν μιᾷ τῶν πόλεων (5:12a) and it is separated from the next succeeding block of three units transferred (Lk 5:17-39 = Mt 9:1-17) by 5:17a (καὶ ἐγένετο ἐν μιᾷ τῶν ἡμερῶν). Further these three units are separated from the next transferred unit (Lk 6:1-5) by an editorial note of time (Ἐγένετο δὲ ἐν σαββάτῳ [δευτεροπρώτῳ]). Yet the three units are intimately linked with each other chronologically even more closely than in Matthew. For Luke links The Healing of the Paralytic with the Call of Levi by the phrase μετὰ ταῦτα, and the Call of Levi with the Question of Fasting by οἱ δὲ εἶπαν πρὸς αὐτόν (v. 33), which contrasts strongly with his studiously vague introduction to the three units καὶ ἐγένετο ἐν μιᾷ τῶν ἡμερῶν (v. 17). Thus 5:12a and 5:17a are two important indicators that these passages have changed context; and the same applies to 6:1a. In the two remaining units of Luke's First Preaching Tour (Mt 12:1-14 = Lk 6:1-11), Luke gives in each case a more specific chronological reference that Matthew, viz. 6:1a ἐγένετο δὲ ἐν σαββάτῳ (δευτεροπρώτῳ) and in 6:6a ἐγένετο δὲ ἐν ἑτέρῳ σαββάτῳ. Luke in fact deliberated climaxes the Tour by the transference of these two Sabbath units, leading as they do in both Gospels to overt action against Jesus, Mt 12:14 = Lk 6:11. Finally as regards the Baptist's Envoys unit and Jesus' Reply (Lk 7:18-35 = Mt 11:2-19), we again find Luke prefacing them with a more circumstantial introduction, 7:18, and concluding with another editorial passage, 7:35. The more closely the text of Luke is studied the clearer it becomes that one of his main objects in effecting all these transfers (including the Parables' units) was to

reveal the evolution of events that led up to the decisive moments of the Galilean Ministry, viz. the Great Sermon and The Sending Out of the Twelve, 9:7-9.

55. These exceptions, dismembered though they are from their Matthean context, are in fact, re-located by Luke with great care and intelligence. Luke transfers them from one Discourse to another in the following cases: (1) Sayings from three different Matthean Discourses are brought together by Luke and attached to the conclusion of his Parables' Discourse (Lk 8:16-18), namely, (a) Lk 8:16, 'No one having lit a lamp. . . '; this verse is parallel to Mt 5:15, and could stem from the Great Sermon (First Discourse); it is also parallel to Lk 11:33 = Mk 4:22; (b) Lk 8:17 is similarly parallel to Mt 10:26 (Missionary Discourse); it is also parallel to Lk 12:2 and Mk 4:22; (c) Lk 8:18 is parallel to Mt 13:12-14 (Parables' Discourse) and to Mk 4:24-25. (See also *The Fourfold Gospel Synopsis*.) (2) Mt 10:17-22 in the Missionary Discourse, is found appositely in Luke's Eschatological Discourse at Lk 21:12-16. (3) Luke introduces into his own special Last Supper Discourse (Lk 22:21-38) some material additional to Matthew, but we also find there the substance of the following verses of Matthew, which are missing in the corresponding passages where Luke is parallel to Matthew, namely, Mt 26:21-23 = Lk 22:21-23; Mt 20:24-28 = Lk 22:24-26; Mt 19:28 = Lk 22:28; Mt 26:33-35 = Lk 22:33; and also compare Lk 22:31-32, a special prayer for Peter's faith, with Mt 16:18, which Luke omits. That is to say that Luke has enlarged the Matthean account of Jesus' words at the Last Supper into a 'seventh' Discourse by using special material together with these verses taken from the intervening chapters, namely Mt 19—22, 26, i. e. from passages before and after Matthew's last two Discourses. (4) The transfer of Mt 18:3 to Lk 18:17. This would seem to be an exception to the rule that Luke always transfers material from Matthew's Discourses either to another Discourse or to the Central Section. The exception is more apparent than real, if account be taken of the fact that Mt 18:5-6 is almost a doublet of Mt 19:13-15. The transfer has probably only been made because Lk 18:17 is already in direct parallel with Mt 19:13-15. (5) There might also be another exception if the Lukan Parable of the Pounds (Lk 19:11-27) is to be equated with Matthew's Parable of the Talents (Mt 25:14-30). But it is more likely that Luke's Parable is a substitute for Matthew's and that he is also following his usual practice of removing any glaring contrast with Matthew to another unobtrusive context, in the present instance to that part of the Journey Section next to the Central Section. (6) Mt 24:37f = Lk 21:34-36.

56. The Omission by Luke of Matthean material seems to fall into one or other of the following categories: (1) Material of interest principally to Christian Jews living in the Palestinian situation described in

Acts, e. g. Mt 4:13-17; 5:19-24, 33-37; 6:5-8, 14-18; 10:23; 12:16b-21; 13:14-15, 50-52; 15:1-20; 17:10-13, 24-27; 19:3-9, 10-12; 21:14-17, 28-32; 23:2b-3, 8-10, 15-22, 32; 24:20; 27:62-66. (2) Sayings offensive to Gentiles, e. g. Mt 7:6; 18:16-20. (3) Sayings seemingly contradictory to the Universal Mission of the Church, Mt 10:5-6; 15:21-28, cf. Acts 1:8. (4) Sayings aimed at the hypocrisy of the pre-70 A. D. Pharisees, Mt 6:1-8; 23:13-36; (though Luke does in fact include some parallel material at 11:42-52 and 20:45-47). (5) Sayings likely to cause scandal to literal-minded Gentiles, Mt 5: 29-30; 18:8-9; 19:10-12. (6) Obscure Sayings, including Jewish casuistry, Mt 15:1ff. (7) Stories seemingly derogatory to the Twelve or to Peter, or likely to cause disedification, Mt 14:22-33; 16:22-23. (8) A certain number of editorial or linking passages, e. g. Mt 9: 35-38; 14:34-36; 15:29-31; 19:1-2; 21:10-11. (9) Doublets, e. g. Mt 5:27-28; 9:27-31; 13:24-30, 36-42, 43-50; 14:3-12; 15:32-39; 21:18-22; 22:1-12; 25:14-30; 26:6-13; 27:3-10 (cf. Acts 1:17-20); 27:27-31. (10) Omission, by reason of redundancy or lack of space, of a parable or story, but retaining the moralising conclusion that illustrates it, e. g. Mt 18:35 = cf. Lk 17:4; Mt 20:16 = Lk 13. 30. There still remain a few Lukan omissions unaccounted for under any of the above headings. The chief among them seem to be Mt 11:28-30, Mt 21:10-11, 14-17, and 25:31-46, the moral of which however is admirably given an alternative form in Lk 10:29-37.

CHAPTER EIGHT

57. H. J. Chapman believed that a thorough inspection of the Centurion's Slave pericope proves— (1) that Luke used our Greek Matthew; (2) that Luke had additional material to insert; (3) that it well illustrated his thesis that passages attributed to 'Q' (see his page 96) are either almost identical in wording with Matthew, or else that they are so far apart as to the Greek words that they clearly had no common source; i. e. they cannot come from 'Q'; (4) that Luke reverenced Matthew, following it word for word, his insignificant alterations being merely intended to make the sentences more explicit, smooth and clear. . . He also uses it to correct and amplify his own sources. . He is anxious not to lose a bit of Matthew. (*Matthew, Mark and Luke*, pp. 104-5)
58. B. C. Butler, 'St Luke's Debt to St Matthew', *Harvard Theological Review* 32 (1939) 255-6.
59. A Farrer, 'On Dispensing with "Q" ', in *New Testament Studies*, ed. D. E. Nineham, 1957, p. 66.

CHAPTER NINE

60. We accept as relatively certain the view that the Resurrection Narrative of Mark, Mk 16:9-20, although it has solid attestation from the

majority of the earliest manuscript witnesses, has a source different from that of the rest of the Gospel.

61. Thus Chart I enables one to pick out at a glance most of the unit-relationships involved, i. e. the 'Triple Tradition' units, indicated by the straight lines (plain and hatched) linked by the Lukan titles down the middle of the Chart; the Mt-Lk parallels (the 'Q' units) are indicated by the parallel or diagonal plain lines and by the broken lines, the Lk-Mk unites are joined together by the shorter hatched lines, and the Mt-Mk units are joined by the long hatched lines. The units peculiar to each Gospel have of course no communicating lines. Certain items, e. g. the Entry into Jerusalem, the Last Supper, and the Trial of Jesus before the High Priest, present special problems in regard to visual presentation as the result of Luke following a different sequence from Matthew and Mark; but broadly speaking the picture offered is just. Note that I have diverged slightly from Aland's pericope divisions in some, including the following cases, §§99, 254, 269, 293, 332, 333, 339, 340, 341, 347.

62. Since these editorial units all occur in the identical sequence in each Gospel, they go a long way to confirming that the literary inter-connection between the Synoptics is direct, i. e. via the Gospels in their edited state, and not merely through prior collections of material from which they were later put together. In other words, either our Mark was used by Luke and Matthew, or Mark used both.

63. Apart from the examples listed in this §4 (A) there are other examples of Mark's support of Matthew's order both absolutely and relatively, where Luke does not, within the groups of units spanning the Last Supper and the Jewish Trial of Jesus, e. g. the sequence of Peter's Denials and of the Rending of the Temple Veil; these cannot be illustrated without breaking down existing units still further. Nevertheless the general pattern remains identical, Mark agreeing with Matthew while Luke's sequence diverges within a larger pattern of total agreement of sequence. Aland's synopsis arrangement is not however very helpful at these points.

64. I have not included KA 152 (Jesus Heals a Deaf Mute and Many Others) in this category, though Aland does; because although the sequence is the same the likeness is too vague. Hence I have put it into §8.

65. There are two other important items which might seem at first sight to qualify for consideration in §9:

    Peter tries to walk on the Water   Mt 14:28-31
    Christ's Promise to Peter   Mt 16:17-19

However, each on closer examination is seen to form an integral part of a larger unit (see KA 147 and 158) and therefore does not qualify as subject-matter for this stage of our investigation. However, to take the latter case as an example, it is quite possible that Luke omitted Mt 16:17-19 because he believed it belonged elsewhere (cf. his treatment of Mt 8:11-12). O. Cullmann (*Peter, Disciple, Apostle, Martyr*, English ed. 1962 paperback, p. 217) thinks that it belongs in fact to the Passion Story. If this is so, then it is easily understandable why Luke omitted it when editing Mt 16:13-20. For as he already had another Saying of the Lord about Peter's special place among the Twelve at Lk 22:31-32, he did not in this case place it elsewhere, e. g. in the Passion Narrative, but simply omitted it, knowing that it was already recorded in the First Gospel in a suitable context.

CHAPTER TEN

66. There is no general agreement about the main divisions in the Gospel of Mark, as may be seen from a glance at any of the standard commentaries. No apology is therefore made for suggesting another set, which at least corresponds to literary divisions. Each division contains between 1500 and 2800 words.
67. See Farmer's brilliant account of the redaction of Lk 21 in *The Synoptic Problem*, pp. 271-8. Farmer concludes: '. . . It is possible to describe Mark's version of the apocalyptic discourse as a revision of Luke's, in which the general shape of Luke's version of the discourse was preserved, but in which the text was revised to bring it into accord with the text of Matthew, from which Luke's text was originally derived. . . Mark's ending of the discourse (13:33-37) affords further evidence of the secondary character of this Gospel in comparison with Matthew and Luke.' (p. 278)
68. The best study of this Markan phenomenon from the Two-Document Hypothesis standpoint is to be found in F. Neirynck, 'Duplicate Expressions in the Gospel of Mark' in *Eph. Theol. Lov.*, 48 (1972) 150-209; this study was republished in the same year in his *Duality in Mark*, Leuven 1972. Neirynck lists in all 205 such expressions.

CHAPTER ELEVEN

69. Thus in Aland's Synopsis the parallel account of the Cleansing of the Temple is repeated in large type, §§271, 273. This repetition of course has the advantage of throwing back on the reader the onus of deciding which of the accounts go together in parallel, but it also obscures the significance of Matthew's departure from Mark (or Mark's departure from Matthew). Again in Sparks' Synopsis we find the Markan and Lukan accounts paralleled in large type in his §198, although they are not parallel in sequence. The clearest and best arrangement, and the one with which in general we concur, is that of A. Huck (6th ed., 1926, §§198-201). For Huck has so spaced out

the three Gospel parallels as to minimise the dislocation to the actual sequence, and he properly places the Markan Cleansing in the only place it can fit, i. e. between the Cursing of the Figtree and the Discovery that it has withered from the root (see his §§ 199, 200, 201).

70. According to the Two-Document Hypothesis, however, Luke will have followed Mark's sequence (since there is no intervening matter to prevent us putting Luke's Cleansing opposite Mark's instead of opposite Matthew's), and hence there would be no exception to the assertion that Matthew and Luke never agree against Mark. Nevertheless if on other grounds we are sure that Luke used and was following Matthew, we are justified in pursuing our investigations on these lines. For other disagreements of Mark with both Luke and Matthew see Sanders' article in *New Testament Studies* 15, pp. 249-261.

71. *A Hebrew Translation of the Gospel of Mark,* Jerusalem, Dugith, no date, pp.30ff.

72. This view is strongly maintained by John L. McKenzie in his Commentary on the Gospel according to Matthew in the *Jerome Biblical Commentary, in loc.* He refutes K. Stendahl's claim that the oft-quoted reference to T. Issachar (5:2[Apot. 2, 327]) is a true parallel to Jesus' pronouncement, cf. K. Stendahl, Comm. on Matthew *in loc.*, in *Peake's Commentary,* 2nd ed., 1962. H. Wansbrough, also commenting on Matthew, in *A New Catholic Commentary*, 1969, agrees with McKenzie about the originality of Jesus here.

CHAPTER TWELVE

73. The following considerations are offered in explanation and justification of this assumption: (1) Since the writings of P. Carrington and L. Bouyer, it is becoming generally accepted that the earliest Christian liturgy is mainly a development of the Synagogue liturgy as practised by Jesus and his Apostles, *mutatis mutandis.* For the Church always used the Jewish Calendar, based her Eucharistic Rite on the Jewish Passover, and took over the LXX version of the Jewish Scriptures and especially those Old Testament passages prophetical of Christ, cf. Acts 15:21, 17:11. In fact all the most ancient manuscripts of the Gospels are specially marked for reading in the Christian assembly, see Goulder, *Midrash and Lection in Matthew,* Part I, chap. 9. (2) From this it follows that the Gospels were evolved by the Church to meet the need for information about Jesus in the Christian assembly, which wanted to hear (a) how Jesus fulfilled the Old Testament prophecies, and (b) what he said and did. (3) Carrington rightly observes that given these postulates 'it is not realistic thinking. . . (to hold) the curious assumption that personal contact with the first generation disciples mysteriously ceased at some primary stage before the Gospel material took standardised oral or written form; or, alternatively, that any reliable memory of the life

and teaching of Jesus had been erased from their minds. . . Oral tradition was not unorganised conversation or casual reminiscence, provided by unnamed and unknown preachers working without any control; or else the work of local teachers in undocumented non-apostolic churches manipulating material the origin of which was obscure' (P. Carrington, *According to Mark*, p. 12). On the contrary it was the professional and well-tested method of preserving accurate knowledge about important men. Therefore the earliest Gospel materials were created in a Jewish Christian community with its continuous history from pre-Christian times and with its living tradition. This tradition is at all times embodied in *persons*, not in anonymous communities. Hence the Gospels are fundamentally the written version of this well-known oral tradition, that of Peter, of Paul (Luke), and of the Jerusalem Church (?the Church of Matthew). Hence not only the actual text, *but also its omissions* are fully 'explained when the document is correctly placed in its functional and operative position in the continuous evangelical and liturgical life of the Church, and in its relation to other documents of the period with which it has an affinity' (op. cit., p. 267).

74. 'Chez Marc, l'absence du Sermon (sur la Montagne) résulte d'une omission (cf. L. Vaganay, 'L'Absence du Sermon sur la Montagne chez Marc', *Revue Biblique* 58 (1951) 5-46; L. Cerfaux, 'La Mission de Galilée dans la tradition synoptique', *Eph. Theol. Lov.*, 1951)', quoted by J. Dupont, *Les Béatitudes*, 1st ed., 1953, p. 19.

CHAPTER THIRTEEN

75. For Luke had a habit of developing and filling out pregnant phrases of Matthew, e. g. Mt 4:23 = Lk 5:12–6:11; Mt 5:1a = Lk 6:12-13; Mt 19:1 = Lk 9:51–18:14.

A SELECT BIBLIOGRAPHY

Aland, K., ed. *Synopsis Quattuor Evangeliorum*, 7 aufl. Stuttgart, 1971.
Albright, W. S., and Mann, C. S., *The Gospel of St Matthew*, New York 1971.
Badham, F. P., *St Mark's Indebtedness to St Matthew*, 1897.
Barbour, R. S., *Traditio-Historical Criticism of the Gospels*, London, 1972.
Bea, A., *The Study of the Synoptic Gospels*, London, 1965.
Bleek, Friedrich, *Einleitung in das Neues Testament* (Trans. *Introduction to the New Testament*, 2 vols, Edinburgh, 1869, 1870.)
Bornkamm, G., *Das Neues Testament*, Stuttgart, 1971 (Trans. *The New Testament, A Guide to Its Writings*, Philadelphia, 1973).
Buchanan, G. W., 'Has the Griesbach Hypothesis been falsified?', in *Journal of Biblical Literature* 93 (1974) 550-572.
Bultmann, R., *The History of the Synoptic Tradition*, English edition, Oxford, 1963.
Butler, B. C., 'St Luke's Debt to St Matthew' in *Harvard Theological Review* 32 (1939) 237-308.
———, 'St Paul's Knowledge and Use of St Matthew' in *Downside Review* 60 (1948) 363-383.
———, *The Originality of St Matthew*, Cambridge 1951.
———, 'The Synoptic Problem', *A New Catholic Commentary*, London, 1969. nn. 645-9.
Caird, G. B., *St Luke*, London, 1963.
Carrington, Philip, *According to Mark*, Cambridge, 1960.
Cassian, Bishop, 'Luke after Matthew, but before John' in *Stud. Ev. Texte und Unters.* 73 (1959) 142-147.
Chapman, H. J., *Matthew, Mark and Luke*, London, 1937.
Creed, J. M., *The Gospel according to St Luke*, 1930 (repr. 1957).
de Fonseca, A. G., *Questio Synoptica*, 3rd ed. Rome, 1952.
Didier, M., ed., *L'Evangile selon Matthieu, Rédaction et Theologie*, Louvain, 1972.
Dodd, C. H., *The Founder of Christianity*, London, 1971.
Drury, J., *Tradition and Design in Luke's Gospel*, London 1976.
Dungan, David L., 'Mark–The Abridgement of Matthew and Luke' in *Jesus and Man's Hope*, Pittsburgh Theological Seminary (Perspective) 1970.
Farmer, William R., *The Synoptic Problem*, London, 1964.
———, *The Last Twelve Verses of Mark*, Cambridge, 1974.
———, 'The Lachmann Fallacy' in *New Testament Studies* 14 (1967/8) 441-443.

——, 'A Critical Review of R. Morgenthaler's *Statistische Synopse*' in *Biblica*, Oct 1973, 417-433.
Farrer, A. M., 'On Dispensing with "Q"' in *Studies in the Gospels*, ed. D. E. Nineham, Oxford, 1957.
Fenton, J. C., *St Matthew*, London, 1963.
Fitzmyer, Joseph A., 'On the Gospel of Luke, the Priority of Mark, and the Q source' in *Jesus and Man's Hope*, Part 1, Pittsburgh Theol. Seminary, 1970.
——, Review Article of *Memory and Manuscript* (B. Gerhardsson) in *Theological Studies* 1962, 442-457.
Frey, L., *Analyse Ordinale des Evangiles synoptiques*, Gauthier-Villars, Mouton, 1972.
Gaboury, A., *La Structure des Evangiles synoptiques*, Leiden, 1970 (Nov. Test. Suppl.)
Gast, F., 'The Synoptic Problem' in *Jerome Biblical Commentary*, New York/London, 1968.
Gerhardsson, B., *Memory and Manuscript*, Uppsala, 1961.
Goulder, M. D., *Midrash and Lection in Matthew*, London, 1974.
Griesbach, J. J., *Synopsis Evangeliorum Matthaei, Marci et Lucae*, Textum graecum, Halae, 1774-6, 1786.
——. 'Commentatio qua Marci Evangelium totum e Matthaei et Lucae commentariis decerptum esse monstratur, scripta nomine Academiae Jenensis (1789-90), iam recognita multisque argumentis locupletata', Opuscula Academica, ed. Philippi Gabler, Vol. 2, No. xxii, pp. 358-425. (See Commentationum theologicarum editorum a Velthusenio, Kuinoelio et Ruperto, Vol. 1, Lips. 1794, pp. 360 seq.).
Harrington, W., *The Gospel according to St Luke*, London, 1968.
Hawkins, Sir John, *Horae Synopticae*, Oxford 1909[1]; 1968[2].
Held, H. J., 'Matthew as Interpreter of the Miracle Stories' in *Tradition and Interpretation in Matthew*, London/New York, 1963.
Holtzmann, H. J., *Die Synoptischen Evangelien, Ihr Ursprung und ihr geschichtlicher Character*, Leipzig, 1863.
Honoré, A. M., 'A Statistical Study of the Synoptic Problem' in *Novum Testamentum* 10 (1968) 95-147.
Hoskyns, Sir E., and Davey, N. F., *The Riddle of the New Testament*, New York, 1931.
Huby, J., *L'Evangile et les Evangiles*, Paris, 1954.
Jameson, H. G., *The Origin of the Synoptic Gospels*, Oxford, 1922.
Jepsen, A., 'Anmerkungen eines Aussenseiters zum Synoptiker-problem' in *Novum Testamentum* 14 (1972) 106-114.
Lagrange, M.-J., *S. Matthieu*, Paris, 1923.
——, *S. Marc*, Paris, 1929[4].
——, *S. Luc*, 1921.
Léon-Dufour, X., *The Gospels and the Jesus of History*, London, 1970 (A trans. of *Les Evangiles et l'histoire de Jésus*, Paris, 1963).
——, 'Le Fait Synoptique' in *R. Sc. Rel.*, 60 (1972) 495-6.

———, 'The Synoptic Gospels' in *In Search of the Historical Jesus*, ed. Harvey K. McArthur, London, 1970.
Lindsey, R. L., *A Hebrew Translation of the Gospel of Mark*, Jerusalem, (1971).
———. 'A Modified Two-Document Theory of the Synoptic Dependence and Interdependence' in *Novum Testamentum* 6 (1963) 252-257.
Lonergan, B., *Insight*, New York, 1970[3].
———, *Method in Theology*, London, 1972.
Longstaff, Thomas R. W., 'The Minor Agreements: An Examination of the Basic Argument' in *Catholic Biblical Quarterly* 37 (1975) 184-192.
Ludlum, J. H., 'New Light on the Synoptic Problem' in *Christ Tod.* 3, 3 (1958), 609; 3, 4 (1958) 10-14.
Lummis, E. W., *How Luke was written*, Cambridge, 1915.
Marshall, I. Howard, *Luke: Historian and Theologian*, Paternoster Press, 1970.
McLoughlin, S., 'The Gospels and the Jesus of History' in *Downside Review* 87 (1969) 183-200.
Morgenthaler, R., *Statistische Synopse*, Zürich-Stuttgart, 1971.
Morton, A. Q., *The Structure of Luke and Acts*, London, 1964.
Moule, C. F. D., *The Birth of the New Testament*, London, 1966[2].
———, 'The Intention of the Evangelists' in *New Testament Essays, Studies in Memory of T. W. Manson*, Manchester, 1959.
Neirynck, F., *The Minor Agreements of Matthew and Luke against Mark*, Leuven, 1975.
———, *Duality in Mark*, Leuven, 1972.
———, 'The Argument from Order and Luke's Transpositions' in *Eph. Theol. Lov.*, 49 (1973) 784-815.
Nineham, D. E., *St Mark*, London, 1969.
Orchard, J. B., and Longstaff, T. R. W., (edited by:), *J. J. Griesbach, Synoptic and Text Critical Studies 1776-1976*, Cambridge University Press 1977.
Palmer, H., *The Logic of Gospel Criticism*, London, 1968.
Pierson Parker, *The Gospel before Mark*, Chicago, 1953.
Rengstorf, K. H., *Das Evangelium nach Lukas*, Göttingen, 1958.
Riesenfeld, H., *The Gospel Tradition and Its Beginnings*, London, 1957.
———, *On the Gospel Tradition*, Oxford, 1970.
Rohde, J., *Rediscovering the Teaching of the Evangelists*, London, 1968.
Sabourin, L., 'The Synoptic Problem: Old and New Approaches' in *Biblical Theology Bulletin* 3 (1973) 306ff.
Sanday, W., ed., *Studies in the Synoptic Problem*, Oxford, 1911.
Sanders, E. P., *Tendencies of the Synoptic Tradition*, Cambridge, 1969.
———, 'The Argument from Order and the Relationship between Matthew and Luke' in *New Testament Studies* 15 (1968-9) 249-61.
———, 'The Overlaps of Mark and Q and the Synoptic Problem' in *New Testament Studies*, July 1973.

Schlatter, A., *Der Evangelist Matthäus*, Stuttgart, 1963⁶.
Schmid, J., *Matthäus und Lukas, Untersuchung des Verhaltnisses ihrer Evangelien*, Friburg-im-Breisgau, 1930, (cf. *Introduction à la Bible*, II, 1959, 275-278).
Schmidt, K., *Der Rahmen der Geschichte Jesu*, Berlin, 1919.
Schulz, S., *Q—die Spruchquelle der Evangelisten*, Zürich, 1972.
Sieffert, F. L., *Ueber den Ursprung des ersten kanonischen Evangeliums: eine kritische Abhandlung*, Königsberg, 1832.
Simons, Ed., *Hat der dritte Evangelist den kanonischen Matthäus benützt?* Bonn, 1880.
Simpson, R. T., 'The Major Agreements of Matthew and Luke against Mark' in *New Testament Studies* 12 (1965-6) 273-284.
Snape, H. C., 'The Composition of the Lukan Writings: a Re-assessment' in *Harvard Theological Review* 53 (Jan. 1960).
Solages, B. de, *Synopse des Evangiles, Méthode nouvelle*, Leiden, 1959.
——, *Critique des Evangiles et méthode historique des synoptiques selon R. Bultmann*, Toulouse, 1972.
——, *La Composition des Evangiles*, Leiden, 1973.
——, *Comment sont nés les évangiles Mt, Mc, Lc?*, Toulouse, 1973.
Speaker, Moneta, S., *The Chria in the Synoptic Tradition*: A Thesis presented to the Graduate School at Southern Methodist University, Dallas, 1960.
Stanley, D., 'Didache as a constitutive Element of the Gospel Form' in *Catholic Biblical Quarterly* 17 (1955) 216-228.
Stendahl, K., *The School of Matthew*, Uppsala, 1954.
——, ' "Quis et Unde?" Judentum Urchristentum Kirche' in *Festschrift für J. Jeremias*, ed. W. Eltester, *Z. F. N. T. W. Beihaft* 26 (1960) 94-105.
Streeter, B. H., *The Four Gospels: A Study of Origins*, London, 1927 impr.
Styler, G. M., Appendix IV 'The Priority of Mark' in C. F. D. Moule, *The Birth of the New Testament*, 1966².
Talbert, Charles H., and McKnight, Edgar V., 'Can the Griesbach Hypothesis be falsified? in *Journal of Biblical Literature* 91 (1972) 338-368.
Taylor, R. O. P., *The Groundwork of the Gospels*, Oxford, 1946.
Taylor, Vincent, *The Gospel according to St Mark*, London, 1966².
——, *The Passion Narrative of St Luke*, (SNTS Monograph 19), Cambridge, 1972.
Thompson, P. J., 'The Infancy Gospels of St Matthew and St Luke compared' in *Studia Evangel. Texte und Untersuch.* 73 (1959) 217ff.
Turner, N., 'The Literary Character of New Testament Greek' in *New Testament Studies* 20 (1974) 107-114.
——, 'The Minor Verbal Agreements of Mt and Lk against Mk' in *Studia Evang. Texte und Unters.* 73 (1959) 223ff.

Vaganay, L., *Le Problème Synoptique*, Paris-Tournai, 1954.
———, 'L'absence du Sermon sur la montagne chez Marc' in *Revue Biblique* 58 (1951) 5-46.
Woods, F. H., 'The Origin and Mutual Relation of the Synoptic Gospels' in *Studia Biblica et Ecclesiastica* 2 (1886) 60ff.

INDEX OF AUTHORS
mentioned in text and notes

Aland, K., 28, 30, 94, n. 63, n. 64, n. 69.
Augustine of Hippo, 4.
Badham, F. P., n. 10.
Baur, F. C., 7.
Bleek, F., 5, 19-20, n. 4.
Boismard, M.-E., n. 15.
Bornkamm, G., n. 18.
Brown, R., 27.
Bultmann, R., 21, 22, n. 5.
Butler, B. C., 5, 8, 9, 66-67, 120, n. 12, n. 36.
Carrington, P., n. 73.
Cerfaux, L., n. 74.
Chapman, H. J., 5, 57, 120, n. 11, n. 57.
Cullmann, O., n. 65.
Davies, W. F., n. 34.
Dungan, D. L., n. 35.
Farmer, W. R., 5, 9, 13, 26, 84, 87, 120, n. 6, n. 10, n. 17, n. 27, n. 29, n. 67.
Farrer, A. M., 67, n. 28.
Fitzmyer, J. A., n. 35.
Fonseca, A. G. de, n. 5.
Frey, L., 15.
Gaboury, A., n. 5, n. 15, n. 47.
Gast, F., n. 3.
Gerhardsson, B., 21, 31, n. 5.
Goulder, M. D., 21, 22, n. 38, n. 73.
Griesbach, J. J., 5, 7, 16-18, 39, 43, 72, n. 7, n. 31, n. 39.
Holtzmann, H. J., 7, n. 4.
Honoré, A. M., 15.
Huck, A., 94, n. 69.
Jameson, H. G., n. 10.
Jepsen, A., n. 34.
Justin Martyr, n. 42.
Kümmel, W. G., 13, n. 5, n. 21, n. 28, n. 32.

Léon-Dufour, X., n. 5, n. 30, n. 44.
Lindsey, R. L., 105.
Lonergan, B., 3, n. 2, n. 36.
Lummis, E. W., n. 10.
McKenzie, J. L., n. 72.
Morgenthaler, R., n. 1, n. 40.
Neirynck, F., 87, 88, n. 25, n. 68.
Orchard, J. B., n. 40, n. 45.
Palmer, H., 3, n. 1.
Papias, 5.
Potterie, I. de la, n. 13.
Reicke, B., 60.
Rengstorf, K. H., n. 14.
Robinson, J. M., 15.
Rohde, J., 11, n. 19.
Rushbrooke, W. G., 13.
Sabourin, L., n. 15.
Sanders, E. P., 13, n. 1, n. 70.
Sanday, W., 8.
Schnackenburg, R., 27.
Sieffert, F. L., n. 8.
Solages, B. de, 15, n. 43.
Sparks, H. F. D., 94, n. 69.
Speaker, Moneta S., 33.
Stendahl, K., 111, n. 51.
Streeter, B. H., 5, 8, 87, 120, n. 10, n. 21, n. 24, n. 27, n. 33.
Styler, G. M., n. 28, n. 36.
Taylor, R. O. P., 31-34.
Thompson, P. J., n. 51.
Tischendorf, L. F. K. von, 13.
Turner, N., n. 27.
Vaganay, L., 112, n. 74.
Wansbrough, H., n. 72.
Wenham, D., 15, n. 30.
Wink, W., 9, n. 17.
Woods, F. H., 12, n. 20.

CHARTS

CHART I : Unit-Sequence Comparison of Matthew-Luke-Mark

CHART IIA : The Great Sermon

CHART IIB : Central Section of Luke with Matthean Parallels

CHART IIA   THE GREAT SERMON

§ BO	Matthew ch:v	MATTHEW	LUKE	Luke Main Struct.	Luke Central Sect.	Mark
59	5:2-12	The Beatitudes	Four Beatitudes	6:20-23		
60			Four Woes	6:24-26		
61	5:13	'Salt of the Earth'	Parable of Salt		14:34-35	
62	5:14-16	Light of the World				
...	5:15	On not hiding the Light	On not hiding the Light	(8:16)	11:33	(4:21)
63	5:17-20	Christ and the Law	The Law and the Kingdom		16:17	
64	5:21-24	On Murder and Anger				
65	5:25-26	On Agreement with Accuser	On Agreement with Accuser		12:57-59	
66	5:27-29	On Controlling Wrong Desire				
...	5:30	Cut off Offending Member				9:43
67	5:31-32	On Divorce	On Divorce		16:18	
68	5:33-37	On Oaths				
...	5:38-42	On Retaliation	On Love of Enemies	6:27-28		
69			On Retaliation	6:29-30		
70			Golden Rule of Conduct	6:31		
71	5:43-48	On Love of Enemies	On Love of Enemies	6:32-36		
72	6:1-4	On Almsgiving				
73	6:5-8	How not to Pray				
74	6:9-13	The Lord's Prayer	The Lord's Prayer		11:1-4	
75	6:14-15	Forgive and be Forgiven				11:25-26
76	6:16-18	On Fasting				
77	6:19-21	On Treasures in Heaven	On Treasures in Heaven		12:33-34	
78	6:22-23	The Sound Eye	The Sound Eye		11:34-36	
79	6:24	On Serving Two Masters	On Serving Two Masters		16:13	
80	6:25-34	On Temporal Anxieties	On Temporal Anxieties		12:22-31	
81	7:1-5	On Judging Others	On Judging Others	6:37-42		
82	7:6	'Guard what is Holy'				
83	7:7-11	On Asking God	Encouragement to Pray		11:9-13	
84	7:12	Golden Rule of Conduct				
85	7:13-14	The Two Ways	Warning re Exclusion f. Kgdm		13:23-24	
86	7:15-20	A Tree known by Fruits	A Tree known by Fruits	6:43-45		
87	7:21-23	On Doing the Word	On Doing the Word	6:46	13:25-27	
88	7:24-27	Parable of House b. on Rock	Parable of House b. on Rock	6:47-49		(4:24b)

CHART IIB — CENTRAL SECTION OF LUKE with Matthean Parallels

§ BO	Luke Central Section Unit Titles	Discourse Matthew Luke C/S	1 5–7 (6:20-49)	8–9	2 10 (9:3-5)	11,12	3 13 (8:4-18)	14–17	4 18 (9:46-48)	19–22	5 23 (20:45-47)	6 24, 25 (21:5-36)	Mark
203	Samaritan Village refuses Jesus	*9:52-56											
204	On Following Jesus	9:57-62		8:18-22									
205	'The Harvest is Great...'	10:1-2		9:37-38									
...	Mission of the Seventy (two)	10:3-12			10:7-16								
206	Woes on Unrepentant Cities	10:13-15				11:20-24							
207	'He who hears you hears Me'	10:16			(10:40)								
208	Return of the Seventy (two)	*10:17-20											
209	Thanksgiving of Jesus	10:21-22				11:25-27							
210	'Blessed your Eyes'	10:23-24					13:16-17						
211	The Lawyer's Question	10:25-28								22:34-40			12:28-34
212	Parable of the Good Samaritan	*10:29-37											
213	Visit to Martha and Mary	*10:38-42											
214	The Lord's Prayer	11:1-4	6:9-13										
215	The Importunate Friend	*11:5-8											
216	Encouragement to Pray	11:9-13	7:7-11										
217	Healing of Dumb Man	11:14				(cf. 12:22-23)							
...	Jesus and Beelzebul	11:15-23				12:24-30							3:22-27
218	Return of the Unclean Spirit	11:24-26				12:43-45							
219	The Truly Blessed	*11:27-28											
220	The Sign of Jonah	11:29-32				12:38-42							
221	Concerning Light	11:33	5:15										4:21=Lk 8:16
222	The Sound Eye	11:34-36	6:22-23										
223	Woes agst Pharisees & Lawyers	11:37-54								23:4-36			
224	Leaven of the Pharisees	12:1						16:5-6					8:14-15
225	Exhortation to Fearless Confes.	12:2-9			10:26-33								
226	Sin against the Holy Spirit	12:10				12:31-32							3:28-30
227	Assistance of the Holy Spirit	12:11-12			10:19-20								13:11
228	Warning against Avarice	*12:13-15											
229	Parable of the Rich Fool	*12:16-21											
230	On Anxieties re Earthly Things	12:22-32	6:20-24										
231	Treasures in Heaven	12:33-34	6:19-21										

Denotes pericopes proper to Luke.

	Title	Luke					Matthew
232	Watching with Lamps Lit	12:35-38					25:1-13
233	Parable of Thief in the Night	12:39-40					24:42-44
234	Parable of W. & F. Steward	12:41-48					24:45-51
235	Jesus, Divider of Households	12:49-53		10:34-36			
236	Interpreting Signs of the Times	12:54-56	16:2-3				
237	On Agreement with One's Accuser	12:57-59	5:25-26				
238	Repentance or Destruction	*13:1-5					
239	Parable of the Barren Figtree	*13:6-9					
240	Healing of a Crippled Woman	13:10-17					
241	Parable of the Mustard Seed	13:18-19			13:31-32		4:30-32
242	Parable of the Leaven	13:20-21			13:33		
243	Warning of Exclus. from Kgdm	13:22-24	7:13-14				
		13:25-27	7:22-23				(25:10-12)(13:35)
...	'I know you not...'	13:28-29	8:11-12				8:11-13
	The Sons will be cast out	13:30				19:30;20:16	10:31
244	'The Last shall be First...'	*13:31-33					
245	Jesus laments over Jerusalem	13:34-35				23:37-39	
246	Healing of a Dropsical Man	*14:1-6					
247	Advice to Guests on Humility	*14:7-10					
	'Everyone who exalts himself...'	*14:11			18:4	23:12	
248	Advice to Host about his Guests	*14:12-14					
249	Parable of the Great Supper	*14:15-24		10:37-38			
250	Conditions of Discipleship	14:25-27					
251	Parable of the Tower-builder	*14:28-33					
252	Parable of Salt	14:34-35	5:13				
253	Parable of the Lost Sheep	15:1-7			18:12-14		(cf. 9:49-50)
254	Parable of the Lost Coin	*15:8-10					
255	Parable of the Prodigal Son	*15:11-32					
256	Parable of Dishonest Steward	*16:1-9					
257	On Faithfulness in what is Least	*16:10-12					
258	On Serving Two Masters	16:13	6:24				
259	The Pharisees Reproved	*16:14-15					
260	The Kingdom violently Entered	16:16		11:12-13			
261	The Law can never pass away	16:17	5:18				
262	Concerning Divorce	16:18	5:32				
263	Parable of Rich Man and Lazarus	*16:19-31					
264	Warnings against Scandals	17:1-3a			18:6-7		9:42-48
					18:15, 21-22		
265	On Forgiveness	17:3b-4					
266	On Faith	17:5-6		17:19-21			
267	Parable of Unprofitable Servant	*17:7-10					
268	Healing of Ten Lepers	*17:11-19					
269	On the Coming of the Kingdom	*17:20-21					
270	On the Day of the Son of Man	17:22-37		10:39			24:17-41 13:21-23
271	Parable of Unjust Judge & Widow	*18:1-8					
272	Parable of Pharisee & Tax-collect.	*18:9-13					
...	'Everyone that exalteth Himself'	18:14			18:4	23:12